D1826128

1977
My first year of Epilepsy

By

Glyn Marston

To Roger,

Best Wishes

www.newgeneration-publishing.com

 New Generation Publishing

Introduction

From time to time I return to the cul-de-sac where it happened, where my first incident happened and I try to work out what actually happened that day - the day of my first seizure. I stand there with the vision of that day in my head and I will look for anything that will tell me of what really happened that morning. I still recall (with visions in my head) the residents coming to my aid as I lay on the cold tarmac road, and I recall the ambulance taking me away but I have no memory of waking up, no memory of collecting my newspapers and cycling into the area on that day - the day that changed my life. One morning in August 1977 I woke up in the middle of a cul-de-sac instead of waking up in bed, and I had no idea of how I got there. I looked around and instead of seeing the posters of Freddie Mercury and Queen on my bedroom walls - I was looking at tarmac, kerbsides and houses. I lay there in the middle of the road, feeling numb and shivering with cold (or was it shock?). As medics asked me questions, I had no recollection of how I got there and no recollection of what had happened that morning.

This is the story of my first year of epilepsy, when my life became a world where I was banned from swimming and not even allowed to ride my bike. I was not allowed outside of my home, well not without a chaperone anyway. Imagine being a fourteen year old boy who was used to a life of being active and now suddenly it has all been taken away from you? That fourteen year old boy was me - locked away for my own safety and cut off from the outside world as I was now living in another dimension and in a world where only myself and my family existed and it was epilepsy that caused it. In a time when folk didn't quite understand the condition, I became a social outcast because of the public's misunderstanding and ignorance of epilepsy.

Epilepsy changed my life, it took control of my brain, my body and everything I took for granted. It stole a whole year from me, a year from school and a year of being a happy teenager and even though I successfully received medication within twelve months to control my condition, my life was never going to be the same. 1977 was a bad year for me, as my faithful border collie dog died this year. We had the Queens silver jubilee to celebrate in this year and talking of Queen - Queen were topping the charts with 'We are the champions/ We will rock you' tracks from their 'News of the World' album.

1977 was the year my grandmother died and as I write this now (many, many years later) I can admit with tears in my eyes that I still miss her. My grandmother was a woman that commanded respect, she was the head of the family and we would not dare question her or answer her back but as I have said we all respected her and for me that respect was from the love I had for her. My grandmother even influenced my parents to name me Glyn, they were considering the name Glen but my gran suggested a good old Welsh name due to having Welsh connections herself - and so Glyn it was.

1977, a time that I had to stay confined to my bedroom with my record player as my only comfort, being a huge fan of Queen I did enjoy my confinement at times when I would lie on my bed and listen to my Queen albums but on the whole I was beginning to loathe the new way of life being carved out for me because of epilepsy.

Sylvia Pickstone

1947 - 1961

In 1961 (eighteen months before I was born) and at the age of fourteen, my aunt Sylvia's life ended when she was in an epileptic seizure and this episode took place at my parents house, which was to influence the way my parents protected me, especially my father who would be there to grab my tongue and risk his fingers being bitten off when I was in a seizure. And so, as I was the same age as Sylvia when experiencing seizures, I was scared and convinced that epilepsy was to take my life for sure - my next seizure was going to be my last or so I thought as I was convinced that I was living on borrowed time. I was to take comfort in sneaking out of my home and visiting my aunt's grave in the hope that I would find some inspiration to help me battle my illness because epilepsy was a subject that 'living' folk would never discuss because of the stigma attached at the time, being a teenage boy whom could only hope of finding comfort in talking to a headstone on a grave was to signal how low I was feeling and how scared I was at facing the unknown journey ahead of me - could the aunt I never met give me some hope, somehow?

I was to spend many years hiding the fact that I am on medication for life to control my seizures but in recent times I am pleased to see more groups who are making the world more aware and more understanding of epilepsy. I never thought that I would put my story into words and so I write this story to give hope and encouragement to any family living with epilepsy. I hope that we (sufferers of epilepsy) will never have to witness the feeling of being a social outcast ever again - which was the case back in 1977, my first year of epilepsy.

Chapter one

Happy Birthday

Saturday December the eighth 1976, I remember this day too well as it was my Fourteenth birthday and the day we were moving to a new house - moving house on my birthday!!

I sat on the garden wall waiting for a delivery van to arrive, for I had saved up my pocket money and my wages from my paper round and bought a new bike - a Raleigh 'Tour of Britain 'bike which had five gears and came in a beautiful blue colour, the colour was the reason I chose it. And as I sat there (periodically looking at my watch) I was quietly singing songs to myself and of course those songs were by Queen, humming the lyrics to 'somebody to love ' and 'you're my best friend 'to pass the time away as I waited for my new bike. My old bike, a chopper bike was given to a single parent woman to give to her young lad (the father had run off with a young lady who was their babysitter) and the woman was struggling to buy anything other than food and clothes for her children. I did want to keep both bikes but my parents always adopted the attitude of helping those who need it and so as I sat patiently waiting for my new bike to arrive, "Come on Glyn, give us a hand" shouted my dad as he huffed and puffed his way down our driveway carrying a heavy box.

"I'm waiting for my bike to be delivered" I shouted back, "It's not going to come any quicker just because you're sitting on the wall" replied my dad, "So get yourself into gear and help with this stuff" he added.

"I don't want to move to another house, all my friends live on this estate and our family too" I yelled back as I tried to lift a heavy box. Quickly putting the box down and finding a lighter box I added "How inconsiderate to move house on my birthday, my B-I-R-T-H-D-A-Y" I sarcastically stated.

"How many kids do you know get a new house on their birthday" shouted my mum as she was carrying the lighter boxes that I had missed.

"It's not my house - its not our house, it belongs to the council and anyway I wouldn't want it as a present because I want to stay here" I called back.

"It's only four miles away, a ten minute bike ride so you can still see your mates, if your new bike arrives" laughed my dad.

"So what's the point of moving just four miles, we may as well stay put" I sarcastically replied.

"Oh cheer up Glyn, it's your birthday.. Happy Birthday" laughed my dad as he ruffled my hair.

"NOT THE HAIR, NOT THE HAIR- DON'T MESS UP MY HAIR" I shouted to my dad as he laughed back at me.

I was really fussy about my hair at the time, I was blonde with shoulder length hair that my dad kept constantly moaning about and telling me to get it cut and I hated it messed up. And as I was just about run back into the house to straighten my hair, a deliver van pulled up with my new bike.

I ran down the driveway to take a look at it but my dad quickly picked it up and put it in the back of his van with our furniture, "You can have the bike when we get to the new house" he told me "Now take the dog for one last run before he gets in my van" demanded my dad.

I took Rover (our much loved family pet) to the bottom of our garden and onto the fields that were directly behind the houses in Stretton road, I looked around at the view and felt a sense of sadness as I could see that part of the fields that I once played on were being dug up to make way for a new housing estate. As I looked out to the view I could visualise how the area was before the building works had started, the football pitch that was kept in good condition by a neighbour with a sit on lawn mower - the clay hills that dominated the views were now being erased by the mechanical diggers that were spread around the area. Memories filled my head of being much younger and crawling through the grassed area that had not been mowed, the long grass was ideal for playing a game of army and I would be 'armed' with my long twig that I used as a machine gun.

"RAT- A -TAT - TAT" came the shout from a friend as he mimicked the sound of his gun. "BANG, BANG, BANG" I shouted back as I couldn't imitate a machine gun.

"You're dead, I shot you" called another friend, "No, you are dead - I shot you first" would be the reply from a mate who wasn't very good at hiding despite wearing a camouflage jacket that his dad bought him from the army and navy stores. My brother Audie taught me to ride a motorbike and drive a car on these fields too, well it was actually a 50cc moped that he had restored and gave me when I proved that I could ride it confidently. I became a keen rider on those fields so keen that motorcycles were a huge part of my growing up - thanks to my brother. As for the car, my dad gave Audie a white Singer Gazelle car to drive on the fields and my brother would let me drive it - I was a twelve year old kid and driving a car. My feet touched the pedals, but only if a little bit of my bum cheeks were touching the drivers seat.

It wouldn't be long before a neighbour would call the police and they would come out and stop our fun, but one one day when my brother was driving the car - we spotted a police car driving from the far end of the fields and heading towards us.

"I'll slow down, get ready to jump" shouted my brother as he slowed the car down.

I jumped out of the car and rolled in the long grass as not to let the police see me, I felt like Starsky and Hutch - until I realised that I had rolled into some dog poo. How I laugh when I think back to that day.

Many years before my house and the estate I lived on was built, the area was a colliery by the name of Allens Rough which explained the huge moulds of clay hills that we played on. But this new estate (when built) will be named 'Allens rough estate' in some kind of tribute to the colliery that was once there. Over the far side of the fields was' Brindleys farm 'which had already been sold to developers or the local council who were having the estate built. For me, it was a sign that things are changing in the area but I didn't want to change my life - I didn't want to move away. And after returning our dog to my dad I made the demand of staying put. Having seven children and living in a three bedroom house had become a problem, I was lucky as I had one brother and we shared a bedroom but having five sisters was a problem and we needed the extra bedroom. But I was adamant that I was not leaving Beacon estate - all my friends live on this estate, I recall the Saturday afternoons whereas a group of my dads friends and I would go to the Molineux football ground to watch my favourite team 'Wolverhampton Wanderers'. In those days Wolves were managed by Bill McGarry with Mike Bailey as captain, Phil Parkes in goal, Derek Dougan, John Richards, Kenny Hibbett and Dave Wagstaff were part of the team. I could still go to watch the football from the new house but these memories are linked to this house and not a new one - I guess I was trying to find negative reasons for not moving.

"I ain't coming, I am staying here, give me the keys to this house and give me my bike" I demanded. "This house in Stretton road had been my home since I could remember, all my memories are here and I want to stay here" I begged.

"You can have your bike but not the keys, I have to hand the keys back to the council" explained my dad as he took my new bike from his van.

"Bye then" said my dad as he handed me a bit of paper with the address of the new house, "Feel free to drop by for a cuppa" he laughed as he and my mum drove away with my sisters - my sisters were going to the new house in my aunt's car, they looked back through the rear passenger windows and stuck their two fingers up at me as they drove away.

I stood there with a new bike wrapped in cardboard and began to contemplate whether I should start walking around the corner to visit my grandmother or cycle to the new house and swallow my pride but I had no tools to set the bike up so I knocked the door of our soon to be 'ex' next door neighbour to ask if I could use some of his bike tools and of course he offered to set up the bike for me so I could ride off into the sunset - well, to the new house anyway. While he was setting it up I visited my grandmother whom always seemed to have the kettle on, "I don't want to go" I sighed to my grandmother.

"New house, new beginning" Replied my grandmother as she poured a cup of tea. "Anyway, you are only in Short Heath - just up the road and a couple of minutes ride to come and see me" She added as I supped my tea.

We chatted about my youth and how I would spend every lunch hour from school at my grandmother's house, Beacon Primary school was just across the road from my grandmother's house which was just around the corner from my house, but I would rather spend my lunch hours from school with my gran. "Happy birthday lad" My grandmother said as she handed me my birthday card. I read that card over and over - I loved to receive birthdays cards from my grandmother for it was one highlight of the day for me.

"Remember the time that you climbed on the school roof to retrieve your ball and couldn't get down?" My grandmother laughed "The fire brigade was called out to get you off, your dad didn't find it funny though" She added. "And the time Audie and I were revving a motorbike in the passageway early one Sunday morning, dad jumped out of bed in a rage and chased us down the street - he had ran over three hundred yards before he realised that he had no clothes on" I chuckled in reply. There were a few memories that were hurtful to recall such as a car accident we had when I

9

was very young, and when I was five years old - the day I can never get out of my head was when my mum was giving me a strip wash in front of the fire (having an emersion heater was too costly to heat up for a daily bath and so a strip wash in a bowl before going to school was the routine) my mum fainted and hit her head on the fire grate, the hearth filled with blood and my sister Kate and I thought that she was dead. We ran half dressed down the street screaming "MUMMY'S DEAD- MUMMY'S DEAD" but luckily for us (and my mum) my aunt lived just two doors away and sent a neighbour to the phone box to call for an ambulance while she tended to my sister and I.

As I looked from the bay window in my grandmothers front room I could see the wooden hut that was Beacon youth club, this was a huge wooden building and I spent many evenings at the youth club that was managed by Johnny Landor, a woman named Sylvie and my cousin Caroline (big Caroline as my family called her because my sister had the same name- my sister was little Caroline), Big Caroline taught us to play badminton - Johnny Landor taught us to play table tennis and snooker. Friday night was disco nights at the youth club and I remember dancing to 'Footsie' by Wigans chosen few - I would dance to that with spins on the floor (an early type of break dancing?), Frankie Valli's 'The night' had been given a make over and I would dance to the sound of "The night begins to turn your head around.", such great memories. Now why have two children in the family with the same name you may ask? The answer is simple - Big Caroline was the first female to visit my mum when she came home from the hospital when my sister was born and so my sister was named after big Caroline - it could have been worse, a neighbour by the name of Hilda could have visited first.

My time with my grandmother was comforting for a lad who was stressing out about moving house and I was in no rush to go home - until - looking at the time I suddenly remembered that I had to collect my new bike from my neighbour, "My bike, my bike - I have to go gran, I have to pick up my bike and go … home" I only managed to sigh the word 'home' because I didn't want to accept that I was leaving the estate I was bought up on. After collecting my bike and thanking my neighbour I headed off home but the long way round as I wanted to test my new bike on a longer ride and being the stubborn kid I was, I wanted to get home later to give my parents cause for concern "It'll do them good to worry about me" I thought to myself.

I eventually reached the new house and my dad answered the door, shouting to my mum he called, "Eileen, we have a strange man at the door - are you expecting visitors?" "Not me Roland, I'm not expecting anyone" my mum called back.

"Stop messing around and let me in" I shouted at my dad.

"So you found your way here then?" asked my dad,

"No - I'm lost on the Wolverhampton road and this is an hologram of your son" I sarcastically joked in reply.

I knew where the new house was located because I had sneaked out of school a few days previously to see it, the new house was nearer to my school and meant that I didn't have to catch a bus to school anymore which was a bonus, another bonus was that I would have my own bedroom and not have to share with my older brother because he had moved into a place of his own with his soon to be wife. But when I walked into a small empty room that was to be my bedroom, I thought that it was more of a cupboard then a bedroom, but I reluctantly unpacked my boxes after my dad had built up my bed and wardrobe.

I had no choice but to try to settle in my new home which had central heating and waking up to a warm house in winter was a huge bonus too, I had made new friends and kept in touch with my old friends and life was good, well better than I thought it would be. I quit my paper round at my old newsagents and got another one with the newsagents where I was now living. I was meeting a lot of new girls too and so I was not so sad at having to move. I was making new friends as it seemed that children on this new estate were all in the same boat and that being the fact that we had all moved to brand new houses on a brand new council estate and left our old friends behind. Some of these new friends were from rival schools in my region and making friends with the enemy did seem strange at first. There were pupils from Willenhall comprehensive school, T.P. Riley school, Frank F Harrison school and Pool Hayes comprehensive (the school I attended along with my sister) but as I said, we did become friends but only after we got fed up of fighting with each other.

Christmas was beginning to creep upon us and so one of my new friends had come up with a new way of making some money, John was working at a local independent supermarket and could get his hands on the keys to the lock up where the owner stocked his alcohol and cigarettes , "I was thinking about leaving a window on on the latch so we could get easy access but he has bars on every window" explained John as we all stood there smoking our cigarettes (yes we were all fourteen years old and smoking).

"When the boss sends me to get more stock from the lock up, I will leave the door on the latch so it will be closed but not locked and we can go back later in the evening- walk in and take what we want" chuckled John.

"Yes, yes.. we can sell the booze and cigarettes and make some money" replied Mark "But keep some cigarettes to ourselves" he added.

"Count me out" I interrupted, "Leave me out of this", I added as I stubbed my cigarette out on the floor.

"What, you don't want in?" Asked John,

"No, No way- my dad will kill me if we get caught and anyway, he is a mate of the man who owns that supermarket, they are drinking buddies - can you imagine the embarrassment I would cause my dad if we got caught?" I explained. "My dad would kill me if we got caught" I added.

This refusal to be part of the burglary was followed by chants of "CHICKEN" and the 'BWERK, BWERK 'chicken noises from my so called mates but I wasn't bothered, I was not going to embarrass my dad by robbing from his friends lock up and I definitely wasn't going to risk a good hiding if we were to get caught. And for a few days that followed my friends would talk about the robbery as if they were the Willenhall equivalent of east-end gangsters, they had agreed that the robbery was to be done the following Friday evening.

"Do not knock on my door on Friday, I am not interested" I stated firmly which was followed yet again by chicken noises.

Friday evening came and my parents had gone to the local pub, I was pacing the living room floor and constantly checking the time, "I hope that they change their minds and they don't go through with it" I kept thinking to myself.

"Are you okay?" asked my sister as she could see that I was feeling uneasy and restless, I reassured her that I was fine and eventually I settled down to watch T.V but at around 10.30pm my dad came storming through the front door and into the living room pulling me out of the armchair by the scruff of my neck he shouted "WHERE HAVE YOU BEEN TONIGHT- WHERE HAVE YOU BEEN?" I knew exactly what he was going on about. "I've been here all night watching television" I trembled as I replied.

"He has dad, he's not gone out all evening" confirmed my sister Denise, "Why whats happened?" she asked.

"I'll tell you what's happened" growled my dad as he let go of me, "I was sitting in the pub with Ernie having a drink when his wife came in to tell him that one of his part time staff has been caught with his mates trying to steal stock from his lock up and that member of staff is John .. isn't John your friend Glyn?" Asked my dad as he stared menacingly at me.

"Like I said I have been in here all evening, it's nothing to do with me" I explained as I shrugged my shoulders.

"Yes, but you must have known that they were planning to do this?" asked my dad "And if you did know and chose to say nothing, then that makes you as bad as them".

"Dad, those mates are always talking about doing daring things, they fantasise about being bank robbers and Britains most wanted but I take no notice of it and I had no idea that they would try to rob your mates lock up" I explained to my dad.

If I had told him that I knew and didn't tell anyone he would not have been happy, but all the same, it took him some time for him to calm down over this because he felt that I must have had some idea about the attempted robbery of his friend's lock up. Apparently someone had seen my friends enter the lock up and phoned for the police, the police nabbed them one by one as they walked out of the lock up with most of the stock in their arms - and was I pleased not to have been with them?

Christmas had come and gone, the first Christmas in our new home and we had greeted the new year in style with a family party. Happy new year? Let's hope it is, it can't be no worse than last year could it - moving home and trying to make new friends?

The new year started well as I had a new girlfriend by the name of Jane, she was pretty and had a great sense of humour and hinted on more than one occasion in the previous year that she liked me but I thought that I wasn't in her league so to say. Well I was only fourteen, and even though I was a confident kid - I appeared to be shy around Jane. I was listening to music even more now and because I was given a radio for Christmas, I would be seen hanging around the street corners with my friends with music blasting from my radio. The Drifters were in the music charts with 'You're more than a number in my little red book', as was Barry Biggs with a song titled 'Sideshow', Mr. Big had a new song in the charts called 'Romeo' and David Bowie's new song called Sound and vision was quite revolutionary for its time. However when Paul Nicholas's song (Grandma's party) or Manhattan Transfer's song (Chanson D'mour) came on - I would quickly turn my radio off, "Bloody rubbish" I would moan. I became a reader of many newspapers in my youth and that was because I could read them for free as I delivered them. One story had taken my attention and it was about Gary Gilmore who was executed by firing squad at Utah state prison on the 17th of January, Gilmore had actually requested a firing squad because he didn't want to be hanged. Of course when my dad read the story he muttered "Should put your mates in front of a firing squad for raiding Ernie's lock up".

Since the attempted robbery of the lock up, John was liking his new 'bad boy 'reputation and was getting into trouble more and more- so much so that my dad had banned him from our house. It wasn't long until John had found himself in a children's home for fighting, robbery and attempted break ins, this kid was totally out of control and would fight with any weapon he could get his hands on, after fracturing someones skull with a baseball bat, it was decided that his parents had no control over him and he was now 'put away ' and one step away from going to a youth offenders hostel (or Borstal). I was now a happy fourteen year old, I was earning my own money from my paper round and working weekends at the local supermarket. I was now buying LP's with my spare cash and I had realised that in my singles collection (45's as the old folk would call them) I had every record by Queen with the exception of 'Keep yourself alive 'and so Queen LP's was now making up most of my record collection. I was now wearing denim, denim jeans and a denim jacket - that jacket was covered in sew on badges (mostly Queen) and had the name 'QUEEN' boldly embroidered across the back in red lettering. A few of my friends had joined the punk rock revolution that was sweeping the country, despite the Sex Pistols being sacked by EMI because of obscene lyrics in their songs. I could never understand how folk who shouted and screamed lyrics could become famous- and neither could Jane who shared the same interest in music as I did.

I would see Jane at school and a few evenings if she could sneak away to see me (her dad wouldn't allow her to see boys- she was too young in his opinion). Our relationship was one of stolen kisses when we had the chance and holding hands, we were both very innocent and loved being in each others company.

Back at school, the feared head of P.E was now our head of year too (due to the previous head of year being on prolonged sick leave), Mr Twain was a loud and intimidating teacher and I was not a kid who allowed himself to be intimidated at all - so we clashed on every occasion we met and we would argue time and time again. I had no respect for this teacher and he had none for me, in fact if anything bad happened at school- he would blame me first, regardless of my innocence. Mr Twain had some issues with my older brother (Audie - named after the American war hero and film star Audie Murphy), my brother had left school and started work but he told me time and time again that if I had any trouble with Mr Twain that he would come to the school to sort him out - I declined the offer as it would have been seen as cowardly to going running to your older brother when you were having trouble at school.

I would however, try to wind up Mr Twain by turning up for P.E. and claiming that I was too ill to take part and each time I would come up with a stupid but funny reason to try to be excused from lessons, these excuses included .. 'Hay-fever 'in the middle of winter, and snow blindness in the middle of summer. Of course I would have my P.E. kit in my bag and be ready for the lesson but I just had to wind up Mr Twain before we started- it made the session more fun. I loved P.E. and had a passion for swimming, there was always a sense of freedom in a swimming pool and I had dreams of swimming for the school team and then for the county- this was a challenge that I had given myself and one that I hoped I could fulfil. At school I would constantly be in the head teachers office because of my disregard of school uniform, wearing denim was not part of the uniform but being the clever and cocky kid I was - I knew that at the time, school uniform was not completely compulsory and I would challenge the head to force me to wear a uniform, and so this issue was to go on for a long time. I would spend many hours sitting outside the head teachers office and wait to be called in for another lecture on school attire- while I waited I would read any newspaper available on the battered old coffee table in the waiting area, one story was beginning to grab my attention (at the age of fourteen years, it seemed so strange to been drawn into any particular story).

Despite serious events happening miles away in Yorkshire, Willenhall (along with the nation) was beginning to be gripped in a story that was front page news in all the tabloids - and so on the fifth of February 1977, Twenty eight year-old homeless woman Irene Richardson was murdered in Leeds, at almost the same location where prostitute Marcella Claxton was badly injured nine months earlier. Police (at the time) believed that this murder and attempted murder may be connected, along with the murders of Wilma McCann, Emily Jackson and the attempted murders of at least three other women. This news story was now dominating the stories of British Leyland managers whom on the fifteenth of March announced intentions to dismiss 40,000 toolmakers who have gone on strike at the company's Longbridge Plant in Birmingham, strike action that was costing the state-owned carmaker more than £10,000,000 a week - which is worth a huge £62,500 (or more) today. I would read these stories of Yorkshire and hope that the murderer wasn't a long distance lorry driver with a chance to visit Willenhall whenever he drove past junction ten of the M6 motorway - we don't want anything like this happening in our town.

My days were now a schedule of early morning paper round, school, evening paper round and then 'hanging around 'on the street corner with my mates. and the occasional meeting with Jane. Things were as normal as any teenager would call normal I suppose, the occasional gang fight against a gang from another estate, playing football - I was a great goalkeeper in my youth and I was seeing a lot more of Jane and she would meet me as I walked my dog, it was a great excuse to steal the odd kiss as I let my dog from his lead to allow him to have a run around the field. Rover was a great border collie that had been a family pet since I was two or three years old and his age was beginning to show as he could only manage a fast walking pace instead of his fast sprints around the field but despite this - I always though that he would live forever, a friend for life meant a friend for my life and I could never imagine a future without him but nothing lasts forever as I was soon to find out.

One Sunday morning in March 1977 I returned home from my paper round and as I walked in the house I sensed that something wasn't right. My parents and my sisters were gathered at the top of the garden - the sinister quietness was so strange and I knew that something was wrong.

"Hush, Glyn's here" I heard one of my sisters loudly whisper.

"You have to tell him, he's got a right to know" replied my other sister.

I walked down the hall and through the patio door into the garden, as I stood on the patio I could see my dad digging a hole at the top of the garden - beside him on the ground was something wrapped up, something the size of a dog.

"ROVER, ROVER- HERE BOY" I called my dog in the hope that he would come running to me from anywhere, but he didn't come.

My dad (who was still on his knees and digging a hole) turned and looked at me and quietly said "I'm sorry son, he's gone, he died in his sleep".

"NO, NO, NO" I screamed, "Please dad, please do something, save him, save him" I cried as I dropped to my knees and hugged my dog that was wrapped up in his favourite blanket.

But he was gone and had been an old dog that had probably outlived his expected days anyway, but this was no consolation to me or the family and his loss was to be felt for a long time to come.

I lay on my bed all day and reminisced about my childhood - a childhood made happier because of a border collie, I recalled a day when I was walking him in the fields and a gang approached me and threatened to beat me up, but Rover ran straight back to me and was barking and growling so viciously that the gang ran away. Rover made sure I was safe by chasing after them as they ran off and when he sensed that I was safe he ran back to me with his tail wagging. This was unusual for Rover for he was a happy dog with a great personality and an even better temperament but he did show his mean side if he thought I was being threatened. I could walk with Rover by my side without a lead and he would stay by my side as if he was glued to me - I felt that he was protecting on every walk we had together but what was he protecting me from? Could he sense that one day I may need a guardian - someone to be there if and when I fell?

I cried in my room for a long time and found it hard to accept that Rover had gone, unfortunately for me - my bedroom overlooked our back garden and each time I looked out of the window I would see the rockery that my dad had built as a discreet monument to a wonderful pet. My mum commented on the fact of how bad I would have felt if we were to have lost a family member and would I have needed some kind of counselling, "Let's hope that day never comes" she said. 1977 was beginning to be a bad year but it couldn't get any worse than losing a family pet - could it?

Chapter Two

Absent friend

The following months was to see me come to terms with the upset of losing my dog and gradually the pain eased, this was helped with a visit to the cinema to watch the hugely anticipated sci-fi film 'Star wars', I hate to admit it - but I fell asleep halfway through, it went on too long for me. I was to learn many year later that George Lucas had tried to buy the rights to 'Flash Gordon' but couldn't afford the fee, and so he decided to write and produce his own science fiction film instead. Flash Gordon was to hit the big screen in 1980 with Queen recording the soundtrack.

But back to 1977 and another upset to deal with was about to happen - and that being the occasions that my mum would get out her old metal biscuit tin and look at the photographs within, those photographs were black and white pictures of her youngest sister - Sylvia.

My aunt Sylvia died in an epileptic seizure eighteen months before I was born and though I never met her I was always encouraged to refer to her 'Aunt Sylvia' whenever we had a conversation about her. Kneeling down by the side of the armchair I joined my mum in her trip down memory lane and glanced through the photographs with her. My mums sense of loss over her sister ran deep and the hurt was never going away, my mum would sob and cry as if it were only yesterday that her sister had died when in fact it was almost sixteen years ago.

"She looked beautiful" I said to my mum, "I wish she had lived long enough to have got to know me" I added.

"She would have loved you Glyn, you would have been one of her favourite nephews" sobbed my mum.

"Why's that" I asked.

"I don't really know, even though you are your dad's double and my god you have his personality, his sense of humour and his bloody temper at times I still see traces of Sylvia in your smile, I see her in the way you curl your lip when you are angry but I hear her in your laughter and your laugh reminds me of the happy girl she was. You would have loved her almost as much as I did" said my tearful mum.

Daring to bring on more tears and more upset for my mum, I went on to ask what exactly happened to Aunt Sylvia - I knew that she died in an epileptic seizure but why did epilepsy take her life? And for the first time, my mum summoned up the courage to tell me.

"1961, I had your brother and your sisters to look after, but this one particular day Audie and Denise were at your Grandmothers house and I was bathing Yasmin and getting her settled for the evening. Your Aunt Sylvia had popped round to visit and have an excuse to hold Yasmin who was still a baby in arms" she sobbed as she started to tell me the events of that day.

"Your dad had just got home from work and popped his head into the living room and asked Sylvia if she wanted a cup of tea, she obviously replied yes please. I was putting Yasmin to bed and left Sylvia sitting on the settee, but when your dad went back into the living room she had a fit and may have choked on her tongue" cried my mum. "Your dad tried frantically to save her but he was too late- too late" my mum cried.

"Did she have that one seizure or were there others?" I asked,

"She had many fits, but that one was the one that took her - I watched my sister die and I couldn't do anything to save her, she was fourteen years old, just a teenager that wasn't allowed to live her life" sobbed my mum. "She died at my house, in my living room and I can't get that memory out of my head" Cried my mum.

I stood up and turned toward the door "I'm just going to the bathroom, won't be a minute" I said as I made my way upstairs and sat on the toilet trying to dry the tears in my eyes. It was difficult to see my mum like this and on the days that would remind her of her sister such as Sylvia's birthday, my mum would be so sad. "She was fourteen years old when she died - the age I am now" I thought to myself "it doesn't bare thinking about, the fact that death could take you at such a young age".

I thought that as a kind gesture that I will go to my Aunt Sylvia's grave, to see if it needs a clean up and so I made a promise to my mum that after I had delivered my newspapers the next morning I would clean up the grave. And so the next morning (Sunday) I returned home after my paper round and collected some cleaning fluid, marigold gloves, shears and scrubbing brushes - oh yes, and my mum's crudely drawn map of where the grave is within the graveyard.

"Your Grandmother - my mother, was buried there many years later and the headstone was changed, so look for your grandmothers name too" explained my mum "And don't getting stubbing out any cigarette ends on the headstone - it's disrespectful" she continued as to let me know that she was aware that I smoked.

I cycled precariously to the graveyard as I tried hard to keep my balance with a bucket filled with cleaning items perched on the crossbar and a cigarette wedged between my lips but that was the easy part, the hard part was locating the grave itself. So many graves that were overgrown with nettles, weeds and brambles - it was disgusting how these graves were allowed to get in this state. Sylvia's grave was no better, it was so overgrown and neglected and was in need of some TLC. I spent ages just cutting back the brambles and cutting my arms on the thorns, "I hope I don't need a tetanus" I thought to myself as blood was trickling down my arms. After walking back and fourth to the compost bin with my dangerous bits of foliage I noticed a grubby looking person who was staring at me, I felt so uncomfortable and I felt nervous by the presence of this tramp and this fear was heightened by the fact I had shoulder length blonde hair and I may look like a young woman from behind.

As I started to scrub the headstone I could hear this persons footsteps approaching toward me as his feet made swishing sounds in the wet grass (wet from the previous nights rain), my heart started to beat faster as I looked around to see if there was anyone around to shout to - there was nobody. I was alone in the graveyard - a fourteen year old kid and a scrubbing brush as his only form of defence, but then I noticed the shears and quickly picked them up as I glanced round slightly to see this tramp getting closer to me. "If he tries to pull my trousers down, his fingers won't be the only thing I'll cut off" I whispered to myself.

His footsteps were squelching louder on the wet grass and with each step he took - my heart skipped a beat. I could sense that he was getting closer until suddenly I felt his breath on the back of my neck but being too scared to turn round to look at the person, I shouted, "My parents are on their way here to help me so you had better sod off".

"Glyn, Glyn it's me - John" came a reply from a familiar voice.

I turned to see John, the kid who had masterminded the lock up burglary- and got caught before he could steal anything.

"Bloody hell mate, you almost gave me a heart attack, I thought you were a pervert looking for an handsome target" I sighed, "What are doing here?" I asked.

"I ran away - from the care home, I ran away" he replied as he looked down at his feet, "My feet ain't been dry in days because my trainers are soaked, my jeans are the same and I am in a mess mate".

"When's the last time you had a good meal" I asked,

"Whats a good meal" he sighed, "I have been living off mars bars and crisps" he continued.

Passing him a cigarette I came up with an idea, "Help me clean this up and we can go back to mine and get my mum to lay an extra place at the table - she cooks a good Sunday roast" I told him. As we scrubbed away at the headstone he told me stories of his life in a care home, "It should be called I don't 'care' home" he grunted, "I got bullied by a kid and his mates because this kid is related to the family of a house I burgled" He added.

"I ain't no grass" he went on (grass meaning informer) "But I was forced to tell the staff of the bullying and they kept fobbing me off with words like 'Man up' and 'This ain't no holiday camp, what do you expect' - the final straw came when stuff went missing from room, cassettes and my cassette player had disappeared". John was really getting upset and it seemed that the hard man image was slowly peeling away and revealing the John I knew in the past. We got to work on scrubbing the headstone and as we scrubbed we were beginning to make sense of the carved lettering that bore the names of my grandmother (my mums mother), aunt Sylvia and Patsy Jones. "Who's Patsy Jones?" I asked my friend, "How the hell do I know- I hardly know you let alone your relatives who have passed away" came the reply from John.

After eventually cleaning the grave we made off towards my house and the shock on my mums face when she saw the state I was in, my clothes were grubby and thick with dirt. She was even more shocked to see that I had a friend with me too.

"Mum, John has been helping me with the grave and he can't go home with his clothes in that state, can you wash them please?" I asked in the hope that she would believe me.

"Yes of course, you had better have a shower too John while you're here, Glyn will let wear some of his clothes until yours are dry - would you like to have lunch with us?" replied my mum. The look of joy on John's face as he sheepishly accepted the dinner invitation. I showed John to the bathroom and got some clothes for him to wear, John couldn't believe that he was getting a warm shower and a hot meal and he started to get emotional as he thanked me.

"Just don't take too long in that shower, I need to clean myself up too" I replied as I was in a hurry to get out of the dirty clothes I was wearing. After eating his lunch, John fell asleep in the armchair and it was probably the best sleep he had in ages. "Mum, who is Patsy Jones?" I asked as we sat watching the television. "I don't want to talk about it" came a stern reply from my mum.

"On the headstone it has the name of Patsy …" I went on to say as I was interrupted by my dad, "Hush- I want to watch the news" he demanded in a bid to shut me up. This did puzzle me but I sat still and watched the television with my mouth well and truly shut.

As we watched the television, news was breaking about another attack in Yorkshire by the 'Yorkshire ripper' I could just about hear the newsreader above the snoring of John as he lay fast asleep in the armchair but my dad was suspicious about John and had quizzed him over lunch about working at the local supermarket but John denied being the kid who tried to rob the lock up. As John slept I could still see the look of suspicion in my dads eyes.

"You should be waking him up now and telling him to go home" said my dad as he was still suspicious about the kid who got caught stealing from a local supermarket. I woke John up and walked him to the front door and whispered "where will you sleep tonight?"

"I'll find somewhere" he replied, "I have my clothes washed and dried for me- including my trainers, I feel fine".

However my sister was suspicious about my friend, "Isn't he supposed to be in a care home?" she asked, "He's ran away" I replied in a whisper as not to let my parents hear, "Do you know how much trouble you will be in if the authorities knew that you had bought him here without reporting him?" she whispered.

"Oh well, he's gone now, not my problem" I sighed in response. And though John had left, I was still concerned about where he would be sleeping that evening and I was worried about his safety, a teenager on the run is a very vulnerable child.

The next morning I went to get my bike from the shed and set off for my paper round but I was shocked to see that the lock had been broken off the door, picking up a stone from dad's 'rockery' (my dog's grave) I slowly walked inside with the stone held aloft (fearing that my bike may have been stolen) and I was startled by a shadow in the shed, it was John - he had hidden in our shed all night and was shivering from the cold. "Sorry to startle you mate" whispered John.

"For God's sake, I almost shit myself - How did you get in here?" I replied. John showed me how he broke the lock on the door and then apologised for the damage. I found it easy to forgive him on the basis that he hadn't stolen anything from the shed - he hadn't taken my bike, which was a relief. I took him in the house and made him a cup of tea but he was shaking so much from the cold that he almost spilt his tea.

I tip-toed with him upstairs and sneaked him into my bedroom, "Get in bed and stay quiet until I get back" I whispered as John got on my bed and rolled himself up in my duvet. "I didn't know you were a Queen fan" he called to me as I was about to walk through the door.

"Shut up" I whispered back "If my parents hear you, you will be back in that detention centre". I walked onto the landing "Dad, it's time to get up for work" I shouted from the top of the stairs, "I am going now, see you later" I called as I wanted to let my dad know that I wasn't in bed and therefore he wouldn't go into my bedroom to wake me up for my newspaper deliveries. I quickly delivered my newspapers with so much stress on my mind, stress from the situation that John had now put me in - for I was a loyal friend and though I knew that hiding my friend was wrong, the idea of helping a friend made it the right thing to do (a silly attitude to adopt I know, but friends come first above doing the right thing). I finished my paper round and got home just as my parents were leaving for work. I ran upstairs to see John fast asleep on my bed and I left him asleep for a while but I had to do something about this situation because I wasn't going to leave someone who is know for theft alone in my house with my sister while I was at school and my parents were at work. I asked my sister Denise to pretend to be my mum and phone my school to tell them that I was too ill to attend school that day as I needed to be at home and sort out the situation with John. My sister refused at first but after I had offered to do the whole day's housework - she agreed and called my school to inform them of my absence. "He has to go back to the care home" said my sister as she made a cup of tea, "I won't feel comfortable in the house on my own and I may get a job soon so he can't be trusted to stay in the house on his own".

"I will not be leaving him in this house on his own, God knows what will go missing" I sighed, "But I have to help him until he gets himself sorted" I added. I let John sleep until lunchtime and then woke him up, "Come on mate wakey. wakey" I shouted as I shook his body and slowly he woke up.

After having a wash he came downstairs and I gave him beans on toast and a cup of tea, "You have to go back mate - back to the home" I stated, "You can't carry on like this".

But John was adamant that he was staying on the run and not going back to the home and after he finished his lunch, he left the house with no hint of coming back. But come back he did and I found him asleep in the shed the next morning but this time he had found warmth from a metal paraffin fuelled amber traffic warning light (the ones you would see near a road repair or road works).

After I had repaired the damage that John had done to the shed, he managed to break in again and was lying fast asleep in a sideboard that my dad was supposed to be restoring but it was gathering dust in the shed. John had got himself a sleeping bag (probably stolen) and was lying in the sideboard with the doors open and getting heat from the paraffin light. I crept in and grabbed my bike and quietly closed the shed door behind me.

This was an issue that would get me in huge trouble if my dad was to find out, so I had to make plans and the first thing I did was to lock my bike in (what I called) the outhouse rather than the wooden shed. The 'outhouse' was actually a bin store made of brick and attached to the house, it was secured by a strong door and a stronger lock- it was also located at the front of the house.

Over the next two weeks I left my house by the front door and tried to ignore the worry of having a friend in the shed, if my dad was to find John in the shed I could honestly say that I was unaware of it and besides, John wasn't really a friend - he was someone who lived on the same estate as me.

But within a month, a near tragedy happened when John was spotted staggering out of our shed that was in flames, a neighbour had seen the fire coming from our garden shed and a young man trying to flee the scene. This neighbour dialled 999 and requested the fire brigade who came out along with the police (who also came out to investigate). After seeing the flames coming from the shed, the police stormed into the garden to find John violently coughing as he crawled around on our lawn - being sick and feeling dizzy he had no way of trying to escape from the officers who grabbed him by the arms. John was later to explain that he went outside for a wee in the middle of the night and was unaware that he had knocked over the paraffin lamp as he climbed back into the cupboard and it was only by the grace of god that he woke up before the fumes had rendered him unconscious - he could have died.

A knock on our front door at two thirty in the morning by the police was really frightening and bought back memories of my older brother being stabbed and left to die by a gang of cowards who jumped him a few years previously - he survived the attack but was in hospital for a long time.

My dad answered the door with the whole family standing behind him, "Morning officer, what's the problem?" asked my dad as he yawned and yawned again for the umpteenth time, "We found a young lad sleeping in your shed, well what's left of it anyway" replied the officer, "You may want to look at what's left of your shed" he added.

"Also, this lad claims to be a friend of your son and I want to know if I can speak to him?" Asked the officer.

I peered from the front door and looked at the figure sitting in the back of the police car, "Yes I know him officer, it's John but I didn't know he was in our shed" I answered.

My dad looked at me with that 'I don't believe you' glint in his eyes and after the police left my dad and I went to see what was left of the shed, as he turned to me he said "I am too tired to talk about this now but you had better have answers for me later on". I just looked at the remains of the shed (through a smokey haze) and thought to myself "I am in big trouble now".

Later in the day I had no choice but to tell my dad the truth and when a police officer returned later on that day, my dad made me tell them everything, meeting John at the graveyard, allowing him to come back to my house and fooling my parents into believing that he was afraid to go home in dirty clothes. Of course they read the riot act to me and reminded me that I was breaking the law by giving John shelter, but thankfully the police took it no further. As for my dad, his restoration project was over before it began - I know because I had to help him load it into a skip he had hired to throw away the remains of the garden shed.

Chapter Three

Goodbye Grandmother

It was spring of 1977 when the nation celebrated the Queen's silver jubilee, the celebrations had actually began in February 6, 1977 to mark the day that the Queen had inherited the role of monarch and continued throughout the year as the Queen took on her annual schedule of royal tours, but the most famed of all of those commemorations, took place in London from June 6-7 which was celebrated by street parties up and down the country, my grandmother was a huge supporter of our Royal family but she was too ill to join in any street party and her health was not to get any better.

I recall when my grandmother was taken ill and being the stubborn woman she was, she stayed at home for treatment and refused to go to hospital. I never really knew at the time just how ill she was and I thought (as many grandchildren think) that my grandmother would live forever. My parents were starting to visit my grandmother every evening and I knew that something was wrong, this was confirmed when my dad came into my bedroom one evening and after pulling my headphones from my head he said "Your grandmother wants to see you and soon".

"Does this mean I am forgiven for the shed and the lodger incident?" I asked, "I am still thinking that one over young man" replied my dad "In the meantime, I want to go and see your grandmother", "I will visit her next Saturday or Sunday" I replied as I replaced my headphones and carried on listening to my Queen LP's, but my dad pulled the plug of my record player out of the socket and stated, "She wants to see you sooner rather than later - so don't leave it until the weekend". My dad was a great man, but when he asked you to do something- you do it without question, and so I agreed to see my grandmother the next evening.

I can remember this moment as if it were yesterday, a Wednesday evening that was cold and windy and not the best evening to out on my bike but I cycled the four miles back to the estate that I once lived and to my grandmothers house. I knocked on the door and shook with nerves as I waited for my Aunt June (dad's sister) to answer the door (nerves because I didn't know what to expect). Aunt June kissed me on the cheek and allowed me to put my bike at the foot of the stairs before taking me to the front living room and there I saw a bed in the corner of the room and my grey haired grandmother trying hard to lift her head to see who was in the room. My grandmother was always a strong and active woman, to see her lying in bed in a frail condition was too much for me to take in and immediately the tears just flowed from my eyes and down my face.

"Hello, hello" My gran called in a soft voice "Who is it, who's there?"

"It's me gran, it's Glyn" I quietly answered as I tried hard to hide the fact that I was crying.

I knew that she was ill but I didn't realise she was as ill as this, the most important woman in my life (after my mother) was ebbing away and I was finding it difficult to take in. Slowly walking towards her bed I felt my tears getting heavier and my mouth drying up, I wanted to say so much but nothing would come from my mouth - no words at all. "Oh gran" I cried, "Oh my God".

"Don't take the Lord's name in vain" she said in a voice that was barely a whisper and yes right up to the end she stayed a devoted Christian. "Sorry gran, I just hope a bolt of lightning doesn't strike me down on my way home in revenge" I said as I tried to joke with her. My grandmother smiled back as she said "Give your grandmother a hug son, come on I am fragile but unbreakable" she whispered. I hugged her and she put her arms around me and squeezed me as best she could, "I am so happy that you came to see me" she said as she started to cry and though I was crying- I could still feel the warmth of her tears rolling down onto my cheeks. We just hugged each other and she would try to talk but she could only manage short sentences and so I found myself finishing her sentences for her. We talked about anything and everything and how she (having Welsh parents herself) influenced my parents to name me Glyn "a great Welsh name" she would say.

My Aunt June walked in with a cup of tea which was strange to be in my grandmothers house and have someone else make a cup of tea, the kitchen was my grandmothers place and nobody was allowed to cook, bake or make cups of tea in it.

I sat at my grandmothers bedside and held her hand, my gran was six foot tall and a strong woman but I was seeing a woman who was clearly losing weight and getting weaker. I sat and watched my grandmother go in and out of sleep as her eyes would close and then open, she would smile and then seem to nod off. I could do nothing but weep as the realisation was sinking in and that realisation was that my grandmother was dying. I tried to talk but the right words just wouldn't spring to mind and the tears wouldn't stop as I sat there shaking my head in disbelief and crying my heart out as my body started to shake as I tried to control my emotions, this was too much for a fourteen year old boy to take in - if I was ever asked to explain if I have experienced a broken heart, this evening would be the explanation.

"Gran, I love you" I cried as my emotions came to a head and my tears just came flooding out and the sounds of my wailing could be heard by my aunt in the next room.

My aunt came into the room and hugged me, "Let it out Glyn- let it out" she whispered,

I just looked at my aunt and sobbed "Why, why...?" but she interrupted me and said, "It comes to us all in the end" and she hugged me tighter as I sat next to my grandmothers bed.

"I am so happy that you came tonight Glyn" whispered my grandmother, "So happy" she whispered as she nodded off to sleep again. I was now lost for words and I couldn't muster up a single sentence that would have made any sense, I couldn't put into words how I was feeling at that moment. Perhaps if I were to hold her forever, she will stay with me - forever? I couldn't - I wouldn't accept that she was dying, I refused to accept that I was about to lose my grandmother and so I sat at her bedside and held her hand as I tried to control my tears.

Eventually it was becoming time for me to leave and though I didn't want to go home, I had to say goodbye and as we hugged for that last time I just broke down and my body was shaking as I tried to hold back the tears but the tears would not stop.

"I will come to see you on Saturday- I promise" I sobbed, But my gran was adamant that I was not to visit at the weekend, "I am so happy that you came to see me son, so happy" she whispered, "Promise me that you will look after yourself and carry on being that happy young man that you have always been".

"I will gran, I will" I sobbed in reply.

"Get yourself home now son, goodbye" she whispered.

I blew her a kiss as I walked out of the room followed by my aunt June who hugged me once more before I left. I cycled every inch of that four miles with my vision all a blur from the tears in my eyes, I sobbed my heart out as I realised that my grandmother was fading and getting weak. And when I got home I just sat on my bike in the back garden and cried uncontrollably. I looked up to the dark evening sky and cried out, "Please Lord, don't take her - just give me more time with her, please". My dad had heard me and came out to me, "Are you okay son" he asked, "DO I LOOK OKAY" I shouted as tears streamed down my face. Taking a step back, my dad replied "Hey, while you are losing your grandmother - I am losing my mother and I have known her much longer than you have" He explained, "Now my loss may not be anymore than the loss you are feeling but it is not any less either".

"Sorry dad" I sobbed as my dad patted me on the head, "I'll do us a brew, put your bike away and come inside the house" said my dad as if a cup of tea was the answer to the problem. I had to walk round to the front of the house to put my bike away because we had no shed in the back garden at the moment - I was in no position to complain to my dad about it though, not under the circumstances of why we have no shed.

Later on I lay on the bed and didn't even consider going to sleep, I just stared at the ceiling and tried to take in the situation and the fact that the most dependable person in my life would be gone, and there was no sugar coating this situation - no hopes of her making a recovery, she was ebbing away and I hoped that she would hang on for me to see her again. My grandmother was honest, truthful and reliable, she would always speak her mind - even if she offended folk by speaking her mind. She was unique, sometimes stern but sometimes laughable and whenever my sisters and I were ill, we would spend days at my grandmothers until we were better again, my grandmother would always nurse back to health.

One of her methods for staying healthy was to start each day with her specially made Weetabix with a few teaspoons of sugar, a drop of honey and her special ingredient - "a tablespoon of love" she would jokingly say as she would whisk the biscuits into a porridge.

Saturday morning couldn't come fast enough and I hit my paper round like a bat out of hell, I raced around the route as if I were on a record breaking mission and that mission was to get to see my grandmother as I had promised. I finished my paper round and had a last minute cigarette before I cycled home but as I turned into my street I noticed three cars parked outside my house and these cars belonged to my aunts and uncles, I could see the kitchen light was still on (the kitchen being at the front of the house) and silhouettes of a group of people could be seen in the room. "What are they doing at my house at seven o'clock in the morning?" I asked myself. "Something has happened, something has happ... GRAN... GRAN, OH NO, NO, NO" I repeated to myself as I cycled frantically to the house.

Reaching my house I threw my bike against the wall and burst the front door open, "WHATS HAPPENED, DAD, WHATS HAPPENED" I shouted as everyone in the room stood still and just stared at me.

My mum and my sisters were crying along with my aunts and uncles, I just looked around the room and glanced at everyone who would shake their heads back at me.

"I'm sorry Glyn but she passed away in the early hours this morning" my dad told me as he walked up to me.

Walking backwards, I just shook my head "NO, NO don't tell me.. don't tell me she's gone, not my gran?" I cried out.

My dad reached out to console me but I ran out into the back garden shouting "Don't touch me, don't touch me - leave me alone".

I found myself sitting on the crudely made rockery (that was really the place that my dog was buried) and I cried uncontrollably. My dad came out and tried to console me with words of how my grandmother is no longer suffering and now free from her pain.

"Is he trying to tell me that death is a blessing?" I thought to myself but I just nodded in agreement because I didn't want a lengthy religious lecture on the meaning of life and the reasons of death. Eventually I lifted myself from the ground and sat on the garden bench and my dad joined me, "We have had nothing but bad luck since we moved into this house" I quietly sobbed, "Don't talk silly son" sighed my dad.

"It's true, Rover is buried over there" I said as I pointed to the rockery "And we have a funeral to go to soon - this house is cursed" I continued as I stamped my foot on the ground in frustration. My dad tried to tell me that I was being silly and I had let my emotions take over any possibility of logical thinking. I guess he was right, but I felt nothing but negativity surrounding this house and it was not the homely place that our house in Stretton road was.

After a bad weekend I was not allowed to skip a few days from school - not even on compassionate grounds and my dad was adamant that I go to school on Monday. Jane met me at the school gates and could see that I wasn't my usual self, we made our way to the bike sheds and after locking up my bike and having a quick smoke we kissed and made our way to our lessons. I had double biology later in the day, two forty minutes sessions in a stuffy laboratory .. that's one hour and twenty minutes non stop! I made my way to the bike sheds for a crafty smoke before heading to my biology class - apologising for being late I made my way to a chair and sat down.

"I am so pleased that you have decided to join us Glyn" Mr Watkins called out "We are looking at the function of the brain and how it sends signals to our body, the brain is the engine to our bodies" continued my teacher, "Because without it our hearts wouldn't know how to beat and pump blood around our bodies". Putting my hand up I shouted out "Sir, Sir what causes epilepsy?"

"My God Glyn, you are actually showing interesting in a lesson" he sarcastically replied, "Well for a start - epilepsy is a disorder of the central nervous system that sends messages to and from the brain to direct the body's activities and disruptions in the electrical activity of the nervous system sets off epilepsy" explained my teacher.

"Sir, can you explain that in English please?" I asked.

"Epilepsy is a neurological disorder marked by sudden recurrent episodes of sensory disturbance, loss of consciousness, or convulsions, associated with abnormal electrical activity in the brain" he explained, "Why do you ask?"

And I explained about my mums sister and how she died at the age of fourteen years of age in a seizure.

"Death in Epilepsy is rare though it is known that suffers of epilepsy can die in their sleep but again this is rare too" explained the teacher, "Death in epilepsy may be caused by a fall and hitting one's head or if someone has a heart condition, a seizure can bring on a heart attack"continued the teacher.

"What about swallowing one's tongue in an epileptic seizure?" I asked with deep interest, "My parents believe that my aunt Sylvia had swallowed her tongue and choked to death during her last seizure".

"I think it's impossible to swallow your own tongue, tissue beneath your tongue holds your tongue in place and though a persons muscles become relaxed during a seizure, the tongue hardly moves" he stated to the class.

"So if my mum's sister didn't choke on her own tongue during a seizure - what killed her?" I asked as I hung onto the teachers every word .

"During a seizure, a person may have long pauses in breathing, which can become life threatening, especially if they go on too long. A convulsive seizure may lead to an obstructed airway, which leads to suffocation" explained the teacher as he sat on the edge of my desk.

By now my class mates were expecting a punchline to a long drawn out joke, it was my style at school to engage a teacher in a deep and meaningful discussion then hit them with a punchline. But I wasn't joking, for my parents were carrying the burden of my aunt's death since 1961, sixteen years and I would love to give them the reason to relieve them of this weight from around their necks.

"So Glyn, what do you think you do if you saw someone having an epileptic seizure?" asked my teacher. But before I could answer that question, my mates were interrupting with jokes about epilepsy and basically thinking epileptics are freaks of nature (and to run away from someone having a seizure would be the best option). This angered me because my aunt Sylvia was no freak, I never met her but I know that she was a normal girl who was taken away at a young age. By now the class had turn the lesson into a 'who can tell the best epilepsy joke' and the teacher tried quickly to change the topic of conversation. One class mate seemed to be understanding though - her name was Vicky and though I had a girlfriend, I had a huge crush on Vicky (so much so that I discovered her middle name was Anoushka). I would sit as near as I could to Vicky in every class we shared and at the risk of being called a 'stalker' I would glance at her pretty face and the blonde hair that went down her back. Vicky was the kind of girl who would offer help in class and I would regular pretend to not understand a particular task so she would come and sit next to me and help. On this occasion, Vicky was adding her opinion to epilepsy and telling the class that they were immature in their behaviour and attitude to epilepsy. The rest of class ignored her and carried on with their cruel jokes, and I was getting angry until the teacher interrupted.

"Okay class, let's talk about emotions and how our brain can be tricked into seeing things that we could call illusions" shouted Mr Watkins our biology teacher.

"I have seen a ghost sir" shouted one class mate as he stuck his hand in the air "It was my uncle and he appeared in front of me a few days after he died".

"Did he say anything to you" I asked, "Your uncles ghost - did he speak to you".

"No, he just looked at me and disappeared" replied the boy.

"Rubbish, bloody rubbish - do you think that your uncle will cross the dark veil to see you and then leave without saying anything?" I laughed "You imagined it".

And just as an argument was about to start between myself and this lad, Mr Watkins interrupted by asking me my theory and why I thought that seeing a ghost is an imagination.

I stood up out of my chair and took a deep breath as the whole classroom was staring at me in silence as they expected a joke and not a clever explanation. "I believe a theory that I read in an Arthur C Clarke book and that theory is - the brain allows us to record moments from our lives and they become memories, and the memories that are played back to us as we sleep are dreams" I started to explain. "If we can record memories and play them back in our sleep, is it possible to play them back when we are awake?" I asked.

The classroom was so quiet as I continued.

"Now if you were to play a film from a projector onto a brick wall, you will see an image but that image will appear faintly on the back drop of the wall and at a time of an emotional issue in one's life, the mind tricks the brain by playing back an image onto the backdrop of a real life view and giving the impression of seeing a ghost - I believe this theory" I stated. "That's a long winded way of saying that you don't believe in ghosts" said Mr Watkins "But a great theory and I agree with you". Vicky stood up and started to clap my speech and the rest of the class joined in - making my crush on Vicky even bigger.

I was feeling melancholy but had no wishes of seeing anyone who had passed away - even recently deceased folk, I would have loved to see my grandmother again but in real life and not as a ghost or an apparition. Talking of which, back at home and we were preparing for a funeral and a day I was dreading but a day I couldn't miss - I had to be there for my grandmother and say one last farewell. I had never been to a funeral and didn't know what to expect, I didn't even know if I could keep my emotions under control - I was dreading the day of the funeral, whenever that would be.

Chapter four

Curses and nurses

Remembering the talk I had with my teacher, I returned home and was hoping to tell my parents about the myth that epileptics swallow their tongues during seizures, I wanted to tell them that my mum's sister did not swallow her own tongue and her death may have been caused by lack of breathing or maybe an heart attack bought on by the seizure and therefore there was nothing anyone could have done to save her. As we sat down to dinner I said to my dad "We were reading about brain activity and the causes of epilepsy at school today".

But my dad replied with a quick "Oh yeah".

"Yes and apparently it is impossible for anyone to swallow their tongues even during an epileptic seizure" I continued.

"Impossible, impossible?" grunted my dad, "Tell whoever wrote that book to come and speak to me and your mum, we will tell them about possible and impossible, we will tell them about 1961 and your aunt... never mind, just eat your dinner" sighed my dad.

The pain was obviously still there and it was clear that epilepsy had not just robbed a young girl of her life, it had also robbed my parents of what should have been a happy memory. I decided to give up on trying to tell my parents about the causes of death in epilepsy for I wasn't qualified to push the issue and as they have witnessed the death of a family member, I'm not as experienced as they are when it comes to epilepsy.

I began to think of how I would feel if I lost one of my siblings to epilepsy or any other illness, little Caroline - my sister (who was also called Katie to stop the confusion with Big Caroline) is eleven months younger than me and one month of each year we are the same age - so this closeness between ourselves would be gone forever if anything happened to her. By now I was calling Caroline by the name of Kitty and it was a nickname she liked (Kitty being short for Katie). Kitty and I argued and on more than one occasion I went to school with a black eye caused by a punch from Kitty (but I would lie to my school mates and tell them that I got into a fight on my estate) but despite the black eyes, we were close. It was Kitty who was responsible for me inheriting the name of 'Baby' as in baby brother - she had one older brother and me as her brother, and even though I was eleven months older than her - she still called me 'her baby brother', come to think of it - so did Jackie and Emma who are seven and eight years younger than me.

The days rolled on and we were finding ourselves getting ready for my grandmothers funeral. I had decided to sit in the garden with a cup of tea and just drift away to a time in the past when I was a young lad and adored by my grandmother. I remember my gran as a grey haired woman but in her youth she was a ginger haired girl - this explains the reason that my aunts and uncles were excited about having ginger haired kids in the family (as much as I loved my gran, I was thankful not be be a ginger). There were memories of my grandad too, a bed ridden man who was there one moment and then gone the next, he had died when I was much younger and so his death wasn't talked about until I got older.

One memory that sticks in my mind is the car accident that my dad, mother, kitty and myself were involved in many years previously. It was the 'T' junction of Stretton road and Davies road where a car had shot out from nowhere and smashed into us - the impact was fierce and so strong that shattered glass flew everywhere and the rear doors of the car burst open. I remember glancing to kitty who was asleep on the rear seats and as I reached out to grab her - she shot out of the car and bounced along the road. I was eight years old at the time and I thought she had been killed, and so I sat there (covered in broken glass) screaming my head off. The crash was just a few yards away from my grandparents house and as my parents went with Kitty to hospital, I spent the night asleep in my grandfathers bed that was in the front living room (he was too ill and frail to get up and down the stairs). I felt safe and comfortable in that bed but I was still asking if my sister was okay. Kitty survived but had scars to her arms and legs for a while after the incident. These were memories of our grandparents - always there when you needed them, be it a comforting hug or some reassurance, my grandmother was always at hand… but now she was gone and I had her funeral to attend.

Myself, my brother and my sisters were driven to my grandmothers house and greeted by our aunt June. I was led into the living room but the bed where my gran had been lying had been removed and in it's place was a coffin on some kind of stand and as I stood in the doorway with my aunt Ivy "Go in and see her then, she won't hurt you- you have nothing to be scared of" requested my aunt Ivy. "I ain't scared, why should I be scared of my own grandmother?" I snapped back in reply. "Well go and have a look then" said one of my sisters as she pushed me from behind. I almost fell into the room and found myself standing at the foot of the coffin and looked at my gran lying peaceful in a silk lined box, she didn't look the way I expected and it didn't feel like it was real. "I am dreaming and someone will wake me up in a minute" I thought to myself.

I (along with my sisters) started to cry and it was at this moment that one of my grandmothers neighbours encouraged me to kiss my gran's hand, "It will stop you having nightmares" she said.

"You're a nightmare love, not my gran" I thought to myself.

But as I kissed my grandmothers hand it felt like I was kissing cardboard, "This isn't right, it's not right, who's idea was it to put her body on display?" I sobbed.

"Glyn calm down" snapped my dad in one of those whispers that lets you know you are being told off but not loud enough for anyone else to hear, "Go sit in the back garden with some of your gran's neighbours" ordered my dad as he pushed a can of orangeade in my hand.

I sat on the garden bench quietly sobbing away and taking the occasional sip of my orangeade and listened to the different conversations going on around me, a few folk were talking about the latest news and the brutal attempted murder of a woman in Bradford, on the tenth of July a woman by the name of Maureen Long was injured in an attack believed to have been committed by the attacker who is now known as the Yorkshire Ripper. I just shuck my head in disbelief as I was more concerned about my grandmother passing away, what was happening in Yorkshire was so tragic for many people but just for one day - lets dedicate this moment to a wonderful woman who has passed.

As I sat there sipping orangeade and wondering if I could sneak off somewhere for a crafty smoke, I heard the most stupid conversation ever - it was two old ladies who were talking about my grandmother and the first one said, "Haven't they made her look, the funeral people - they have made her look good?"

"Oh yes" replied the second old lady, "I haven't seen her looking that good for ages".

I jumped to my feet, "YOU WHAT, ARE YOU BLOODY SERIOUS- THE BEST YOU HAVE SEEN HER IN AGES?" I screamed,

"SHE'S D...D..." I struggled to say the word but eventually it came out, "DEAD - SHE'S DEAD, HOW CAN SHE LOOK BETTER NOW - FOR GOD SAKE" I screamed as my dad rushed out into the garden and frog marched me up to the top of the garden.

"Sorry ladies but I need to have a chat with my son" called my dad as he forced me to the top of the garden.

"Not here, not today- you do not kick off today, you keep your emotions to yourself and you keep your thoughts to yourself - do you understand?" demanded my dad as I nodded back in agreement and then my dad continued, "We have all lost a loved one - today is not just about you, it's about the family - the whole family, do you understand?" Bellowed my dad as he tried to keep his voice low.

And again I nodded in agreement as the tears rolled down my face, I'll miss her" I sobbed as I could feel my nose bunging up too.

"Are you going to calm down?" Asked my dad, I nodded and mouthed the word 'yes' as my voice was just a whisper under my cries.

"Good, that's that sorted and by the way- you are staying here to help your grans neighbours with the buffet, I am not risking you going to the church and the crematorium in that mood, the last thing we need is you upsetting the vicar" demanded my dad. It was at this moment that I recall seeing my dad emotional for the first time in my life, my dad was like John Wayne, Clint Eastwood and Bruce Lee all rolled into one- nothing upset my dad and he could take on anyone or anything without even thinking about it. This was the first time that I saw my dad with tears in his eyes and close to crying (I guess he was holding back his emotions for the sake of the family) and I was to realise that this was everyones loss and not just mine - I realised that I had acted selfishly.

I did so want to go to the funeral and be there at the crematorium but I could see that today was not the day to disagree with my dad. And soon after, everyone had left for the crematorium - except for myself and a couple of old ladies who were working hard putting on sandwiches, pork pies and savouries.

"Hey Glyn, I have seen you naked" giggled one old lady, "When you were a baby, I saw you naked.

"And the point you are trying to make" I sarcastically thought to myself.

"If you were to see me naked now you'd probably have a heart attack" I whispered to myself as I gestured to the fact that I am bigger now than when I was a baby.

"Pardon, what did you say?" asked the old lady,

"Oh I said errm, I have changed a lot since then- because that was err way back" I convincingly replied.

Getting fed up with elderly company and conversation I went to the top of my grandmothers garden to have a crafty smoke (a habit that I picked up from my older brother and his mates but one that I would quit - eventually) after lightning up I sat back and looked up to the sky, I chuckled to myself as I imagined my grandmother looking down and shouting "Is he smoking in my garden?" My grandmother would have gone berserk if she was ever to catch me smoking, let alone in her garden. "That'll kill you one day" came a voice from nowhere, and looking around I noticed a neighbour peering over the hedge.

"Your grandmother would be furious if she were to see you smoking in her garden" He continued.

"Yeah, I would risk her wrath too if I could have her back here - alive" I sobbed. "Now, now young man- your grandmother deserves to be remembered with tears of joy and not tears of sorrow" Added the neighbour, "Just remember the good days with your gran and the pain will go away". I guess he was right but I didn't exactly agree with him at the time.

After finishing my cigarette and shoving the butt end deep into the soil (so nobody would see it) I returned back into the house for a cup of tea and the 'joy' of chatting to the dear old girls who were now listening to the radio, is the song 'COLD AS ICE' by FOREIGNER - followed by 'GRANDMA'S PARTY' by 'PAUL NICHOLAS' really appropriate at a wake? My aunt June had returned early to help with the food, she had attended the church but couldn't face the crematorium. My aunt took me to my gran's huge glass fronted display cabinet and asked me to choose something to remember my grandmother by and I chose the three tortoises that were made by Wade. The set consisted of a big tortoise and a middle sized one, followed by a small one - to me this would signal the family I had known and the three generations of my family with the biggest one representing my grandmother, the middle one representing my dad and the small one being me. And these were to be keepsakes that I would hold dear to my heart forever.

After wrapping them up securely for me I made my excuses to leave and turning to my aunt "I am off home, tell my dad that I needed to be on my own and I will see him when he gets back" I told her.

I left the house and walked to the barber shop on the square shopping centre, Mervyn Pearson had cut my hair from when I was a baby, he had cut everyones hair on the estate and folk from further afield. Mervyn had known my dad since they were kids and also knew my grandparents and so the haircut was also a trip down memory lane as Merv would tell me stories of my dad when they were young. This put a smile back on my face and I needed it to help me with the walk home - a whole four miles back home. I was cursing my parents for moving house, our old house was just twenty seconds around the corner and I would be home a lot sooner. I stomped my way home in some kind of anger and when I reached home I put my keepsake tortoises in a safe place in my bedroom before making a cup of tea, tea was the answer to everything in my family and I started to joke to myself about possibilities that could happen in our family such as ..

"Mum, I have fallen off my bike and broken my arm", my mum would probably reply "Don't worry love, have a cuppa and you'll feel better.

"Mum, my brothers fallen out of a tree and broken both his legs", "Tell him to come in and I'll make him a cup of tea".

Stupid notions, I know but we did drink more cups of tea when a potential crisis would hit the family.

I grabbed my cup of tea and walked into the living room, I unlocked the patio doors and stared at the grave for our dog (the rockery) and as I looked on I felt the tears rolling down my face. Walking off the patio and onto the lawn, I looked at the rockery that my dad had made as a memorial to the best dog a family could have ever wished for.

"BLOODY HOUSE" I cried, "THIS BLOODY CURSED HOUSE" I cried as I threw my cup against the garden wall.

"Oh, do you feel better now" called my dad who was standing behind me, "Do you want me to empty the cupboards so you can smash all the crockery in the house?" he sarcastically asked.

"It would save on the washing up" I said as I smiled through my tears.

My dad had popped home to see if I was feeling any better and I hadn't heard him enter the house.

"It's this house dad, this house is cursed - I am telling you, moving here was a mistake" I cried as I started to pick up the broken pieces of my cup. "Don't start that again, this is a new build house and we are it's first tenants - it's not haunted, not possessed and definitely not cursed" explained my dad.

He was right, the house wasn't cursed, it was the fact that I didn't want to be living here and resented the fact that I was losing touch with my old friends, friends I had known since primary school.

"I'll tell you what dad" I said as I wiped the tears from my face, "They say that everything comes in three's, well we have had two of them, losing the dog and now gran - I hate to think what the third one will be" I sobbed.

"Superstitious nonsense" chuckled my dad as he left to go and collect the rest of the family from my grandmothers house.

"Yeah, I wonder what the third surprise be?" I muttered to myself.

Meanwhile at school, I was still getting grief from the head teacher about my attire, Mr Twain had joined in too (well, he was my head of year) I was threatened with detention if I didn't wear a black blazer instead of my denim jacket. "Wear a black blazer or at least a black jacket for school" Requested the head teacher. The following weekend I went to town and bought a donkey jacket - it was a jacket, a black jacket as requested and I enjoyed wearing it to school on the following Monday morning.

As I walked across the school yard I heard a piercing shout that had cut its way through the chatter and shouts of a school playground, "MARSTON" came the shout from Mr.Twain, "GET OVER HERE - NOW" . I knew what was coming next, my new jacket wasn't his choice of attire.

"What do you call this?" Mr Twain asked, "A jacket as requested" I replied, "You and the head teacher said 'a black blazer or a black jacket' and this is it".

"Don't get smart with me laddie" Mr Twain snorted in his thick Scottish accent "I want to see you wearing a black blazer or black jacket that says you attend this school- that jacket doesn't have a badge or anything to say what school you attend" He added.

He was right, the school rules were to state that each pupil wore anything that identified the school they attended, and so I went to the arts centre and painted the words 'POOL HAYES COMP' on the plastic panel that was on the rear of the jacket (at shoulder height). I don't know what it was but I was determined not to allow the school tell me how to dress and how not to dress, I feel that I was angry with the fact that I had to move house and I had no say in the decision - I had to move house against my will and now I will not wear a uniform against my will, I will wear this until the end of term and then go back to wearing my proper school uniform after the school summer holiday break.

School was coming to the end of summer term and the seven weeks holiday was approaching, it was a great time because some of the kids on our estate would scavenge wood from the local timber yard and make a raft to sail on the canal. The game we played was "King of the cut" (the cut being a Black country word for canal- probably derived from the term of having a cut through hills and fields to make the canals).

The rules to our game would be to jump on the raft and paddle to the middle of the canal and then push each other off, the last man standing was the winner- King of the cut. This game was great because the raft would be under an inch of water to start with but as each man was thrown or wrestled off the raft, the raft would be lighter and float better and this would result in the momentum of the wrestling floating the raft away from its original position - we could be a mile away before the game ended. Of course some busy-body would call the police and we were made to go home, and take the raft with us (dump it in a friends garden near the canal - ready for the next day).

Walsall Gala baths was always a favourite of mine, as well as the Olympic size pool there was a smaller swimming pool known as the Brine. The Brine was a warm salt water pool and great to have a leisurely swim in. I would jump on a bus and go swimming three or four times a week, each week in the school holidays - for I was trying to keep my dream alive of becoming a champion swimmer. I would either be at Walsall gala baths or Willenhall baths, Willenhall baths was a routine of collecting a metal frame basket with a number on, putting your clothes in this contraption and then returning it to the attendant who would hand you a rubber wrist band with the basket number on. On every occasion at either Walsall or Willenhall baths, my friends and I would go to the baths armed with our card that showed we had earned our twenty five free pool sessions - but we had encased our pass cards in sellotape - under the pretence that we didn't want to get our cards wet and risk them ripping. The cashier would stamp our cards to signify that we had used one of our free sessions and the stamp mark on the sellotape was so easy to rub off (with a wet finger) - our twenty five free passes gave us over sixty free sessions before someone guessed what we were up to.

There was always something to do during the summer holidays, cycling, swimming, football and sneaking off to the canal with canoes that belonged to my friend's dad (who was a water sports instructor). But again some miserable sod would report us to the police and again an officer would come out to us, "What are you doing lads?" shouted an officer from the canal towpath, "Me- I am doing the doggy paddle officer" I called back from my canoe.

"Less of your lip sonny" the officer replied,

"Well how do you expect us to reply- we are here, minding our own business and causing nobody any harm, and you come out to us" I shouted back from my canoe.

"Well you should have an adult supervising you while you are on the water" the officer replied.

"I'll supervise them officer" called a man who was walking up the towpath, and that man was my friends dad who didn't seem too pleased that we had taken his canoes without permission. After we had apologised for taking his canoes, he offered to allow us to use the canoes on the canal but with one condition - he was to teach us the basics of canoeing and to be honest it made the holidays even better and the month of August that year was a hot and sunny one, the perfect weather for being on the water.

Because of my delivering newspapers, I became 'clued up' on the news - there was always a part of my paper round were I would have to walk for over a mile before reaching the second part of my route and therefore I would use this opportunity to read a newspaper as I walked and I would take in all current affair stories. During 1977, there were a group by the name of 'National Front' (NF) who were rising in support and on August the thirteenth the National Front attempted to march from New Cross to Lewisham town centre. This was met with a group of counter protesters and the police- a violent battle broke out between the National Front and the counter protesters but the National Front march was prevented from reaching Lewisham town centre and it was the first time that police had deployed the use of riot shields on the UK mainland. This event would be remembered many years on as 'The battle of Lewisham'. As a teenager I couldn't understand why there would ever be a battle between folk about different colour or religions. Nevertheless, myself and my family have friends of different colour and creed and as long as we stay united - we will never be divided as a nation.

August the 16th 1977 was the day that Elvis Presley died and the whole worlds female population went into mourning, there was no disputing that Elvis was the king of rock and roll - his music was liked by everyone of any age, myself included. It was the shock news of the year- maybe the century. But along with that news was the news of the music craze that was getting even more popular - 'PUNK ROCK' and a few of my mates were thinking of setting up a punk rock band but only because they couldn't sing and no normal band would want them. And so, for a while we would sing and jump up and down- well shout and jump up and down as we pretended to be punk rockers "I DON'T WANT A HOLIDAY IN THE SUN" we would shout to the Sex pistols song.

For a teenage boy I had everything to look forward to and everything was going great during the school holidays until one morning on my paper round, I woke up in the middle of a cul-de-sac, on the road - lying on the tarmac road. As I looked round I could see a bike, it was mine but at the time I didn't recognise it, newspapers were flapping about inside a canvas delivery bag, 'my' canvas bag but I didn't recognise it. I couldn't muster up the energy to pull myself off the ground - I was paralysed and I couldn't even sit up, so I lay there with my eyes scanning the area until some people from nearby houses came rushing to my side. Everything seemed so confusing to me, how had I got there - were the hell was I?

The folks that came to my aid made a fuss and were asking if I were okay but I couldn't answer, my body was numb and my head was spinning. I was carried to a driveway and perched on a small wall with two women (one sitting each side of me) and both were rubbing my body to keep me warm until someone threw a blanket around me. "Are you okay lad"? Asked a man "Whats happened to you"? He asked.

I couldn't answer, my body was so numb and my head was on another planet as I felt my eyes frantically looking around and trying to make some sense of what was happening. My eyeballs seemed to be rolling at supersonic speed and scanning the area as if my brain was trying to analyse, process and make sense of the situation. I had delivered newspapers in the area for over a year but I didn't recognise one house and I felt that I had been transported miles away from home. I felt that I was miles and miles away from home, I felt like Dorothy in the Wizard of Oz - but maybe I fell off the rainbow halfway to Oz and landed in the middle of a cul-de-sac?

The people who were caring for me were trying to get me to tell them what had happened but I couldn't remember - I couldn't even recall waking up and getting out of bed that day. It felt that someone had deleted a few hours from my life and those hours were from the time that I went to bed the previous evening - till now, I have no recall of that morning. In fact, I remember going to bed the night before (in the comfort and security of my bedroom) and then I woke up in a cul-de-sac with no recall of how I got here.

Shortly afterwards an ambulance appeared and two paramedics ran down the path to me, one was shining a light in my eyes and asking questions at the same time, I couldn't reply - even when they asked me my name, I couldn't reply because my body was numb.. and because I couldn't remember my name. I felt emotional on the inside but on the outside nothing was registering and I was like a zombie, a wide eyed but brain dead being who was a 'living dead' shell of a boy. I sat there wrapped in a blanket with the residents of the whole cul-de-sac around me and then someone suggested that they gave me a cup of tea but the paramedics dismissed it and stated that giving me a drink was not a good idea at that particular moment.

Eventually I was taken into the back of the ambulance and put on a trolley, as I lay there I could hear the mutterings between the paramedics as they were suggesting "Fell off his bike?" "Concussion?"

"I know one thing" said one of the paramedics, "His lights are on but nobody's home, he is totally unresponsive".

As a paramedic strapped me onto the trolley she said "You are off to the hospital now". But I just lay there as my body was still numb and head was feeling like it was dead.

"Oh young man, what has happened to you?" Asked the paramedic as she held my hand and continued to talk to me about delivering newspapers, football and anything else that she thought I may be interested in - in a bid to jog my memory and remember who I am and what had happened. We arrived at the Manor hospital in Walsall and two nurses helped wheel me into the accident and emergency department, having a paramedic and two nurses escorting me into hospital added to the confusion that was surrounding my thoughts of the incident of the morning.

Chapter five

Why me?

And so I arrived at the hospital and was quickly rushed into the accident and emergency department by two nurses, "We have a fourteen year old- name is Glyn Marston, confirmed by a resident of the street where he was found, he seems to have possibly fallen from his bike and fell into unconsciousness, there is bruising to his head" the paramedic told the waiting doctor as I was being wheeled into the hospital.

I was taken straight to the X ray department (to check for any injuries to my head) and then back to the accident and emergency department and put in a cubicle were I lay on a trolley until a doctor arrived, he came and asked me my name and again I couldn't reply.

"Young man, please try to answer me by telling me your name" asked the doctor who knew my name but may have thought that I had lost my memory. I began to cry as the confusion of the morning was becoming too overwhelming, I didn't know who I was and as I hard as I tried - I couldn't reply and I couldn't remember my name. The doctor kept on asking for my name until "G- G- Glyn, my name is Glyn" I stuttered in reply as my senses were returning to me. "Great, great and do you know your surname"? He asked.

"Mars - Mars - ton, Marston" I sighed as I was now recalling who I was and my mind was trying to fill in the blank spaces between going to bed the night before and waking up in a cul-de-sac.

And that's how it felt, as if I had been sleepwalking or aliens had beamed me up to a spaceship and then beamed me back to earth into a cul-de-sac called 'Red Pine Crest', I honestly do not remember waking up that morning- no memory of collecting my newspapers that morning and no memory of cycling into the cul-de-sac. As I lay there I felt my inner emotions coming out in me and the warmth of my tears rolled down the cold cheeks of my face as I pondered as to why I was here "How did I end up here" I thought to myself.

As I was lying on a trolley in a cubicle I heard a voice I recognised, "My son, Glyn Marston - where is he, I'm his father" called my dad and soon he walked into the cubicle. "What have you been up to?" Asked my dad as I just stared back at him. "Home, I want to go home" I cried to my dad.

It wasn't long after that I was discharged from the hospital and being driven home by my dad, and after getting a hug from my mum I lay on the settee and fell asleep for a couple of hours. I woke up with a headache and some dizziness, mum had made me a cup of tea (tea and a crisis seemed to go hand in hand as I have mentioned before) but I refused it and I turned down her offer of cooking me some lunch - I wasn't hungry and I couldn't face any food and so I lay there listening to the radio that my mum had put on the coffee table (she thought it may have bought me some comfort - I don't know why she thought that). Listening to songs such as ABBA''s 'Knowing me - knowing you', LEO SAYER's 'When I need you' and SHOWADDYWADDY's 'When' was becoming too much to endure but I was too numb to turn the radio off and too weak to call for my mother so I just closed my eyes in the hope that I would drop off to sleep. As I lay there I could hear words being loudly whispered from the hallway "Is he okay - Glyn, is he alright?" this sounded like Denise who was talking to my mum before popping her head into the living room to look at how I was.

There were to be some bruising to my head and face for quite a while following the incident of that day which was obviously caused by falling from my bike but what caused me to fall from my bike? A mystery to be honest.

I returned to my paper round after a few days rest but a week later I was waking up in the middle of a road (in the early hours of a Sunday morning) and the first thing I saw was a car headlights speeding towards me. I lay there lifeless, I wanted to jump up and run to the safety of the pavement but I couldn't move (I was paralysed completely) and so I lay there helplessly as the headlights got nearer and nearer. The car screeched as it was breaking to a halt just in front of me - I was almost blinded by the headlights, the front tyres of the car were just touching my body and I could smell the burning rubber from the tyres that had screeched in front of me. A woman got out of the passenger side of the car and ordered the driver to reverse a little. She knelt down to me and told me to lie still until an ambulance arrived- I could do nothing else but to lie still, my body was numb, totally numb but I was grateful to be alive. Apparently, this couple had been arguing as they were driving down the road and only saw me at the last minute.

As I lay there the same scenario was playing out and as before, a crowd had formed around me and someone wrapped a blanket around me and like the first time (almost two weeks before), I was paralysed, numb all over and unable to move any of my limbs, my head was dizzy and my mouth dry - my eyes were blurry and my mind was in overload as my brain was trying to assess the situation. The whole scenario was filled with people talking over each other and words of worry could be heard,

"Is he alive?" called someone, "He's alive, he's opened his eyes" came a reply.

"Has anyone phoned for an ambulance?"

"Has someone phoned the newsagent to tell them about their paper boy?"

Shortly afterwards an ambulance arrived and it was the same paramedics as before, "Not you again" called the young paramedic as she walked toward me "We will have to stop meeting like this" she joked "I could get a bad reputation if I keep picking up boys in the street" she added.

I was unresponsive and my body was so numb that you could have stuck a knife in my leg and I wouldn't have blinked. I was yet again having a ride in the back of an ambulance and the paramedic was asking me questions which were a cause for concern. "Are you taking any substances?" She asked "You're not sniffing substances or taking drugs are you?"

I could hear her words but I couldn't reply and my reply would have been a firm 'NO'! I have never taken drugs - never! I just lay on the trolley until I reached the hospital and again the medics were concerned about my second visit to the Manor hospital in such a short time.

As I sat once again in an hospital cubicle I was being cared for by a young nurse and the occasional visit from a doctor, "This isn't the first time that you have been rushed to this hospital" stated the doctor "Something is going on in that head of yours and I will need to talk to your parents when they arrive to pick you up" he added with a puzzled expression on his face.

My dad arrived (along with a concerned newsagent - Melvin was my boss who became a close family friend) and I could hear some mumblings between my dad and the doctors, trying to eavesdrop in the conversation I was unable to make out what the doctors were saying but my dads answers were louder and I could hear him clearly as he said "I know its in the family but he is not suffering ....." Then he was taken into an office and I didn't get to hear the end of his sentence.

After some hours of recovering on the settee back at home, I managed to drink a cup of tea but still feeling weak my mum had to hold the cup for me.

"Mum what runs in the family?" I asked,

"Legs" was her reply as she thought I was trying to tell her a joke. "I heard dad at the hospital saying that it runs in the family - what is the 'it' that runs in the family?" I asked her as she walked out of the living room, but she didn't answer my question. One question she did answer though was the mystery of Patsy Jones, my mother sat with me and chatted about the old days and during her chat she said "I popped to see Sylvia's grave the other day- three generations of my family lay there" she went on to say "My sister, my mother and my niece".

"Your niece?" I asked in a voice that was still a whisper.

My mother went on to explain how a four year old baby girl had died from a fall, a freak accident that was too painful for her to recall in detail but I was to hear from other family members that the baby girl had fallen from a balcony in a high rise building and that conjured up an image that I dared to even think about.

My days at home were really boring as I was recovering and it was only two days of resting but it seemed like a lifetime and so being allowed back outside was a thrill. I was back on my paper round once more and almost two weeks had past without any incident until a Friday morning when I woke up on someones driveway. As I opened my eyes I saw a man standing over me, "Keep still Glyn and don't try to move" he said to me as he held his hand beneath my head.

I couldn't move anyway because I was paralysed all over. My eyes were scanning the area and sending data to my brain to analyse but as I spotted a canvas bag with newspapers inside I found myself shouting, "NEWSPAPERS, I HAVE TO DELIVER NEWSPAPERS" and then I blacked out once again.

I woke up on a trolley at Walsall Manor hospital, my dad was holding my hand and my mum was sobbing as she sat in a corner. I was dressed in an hospital robe wearing just my underpants and no shoes or socks and this time I was more aware of my surroundings, I knew my name and I remembered what had happened, well I remember lying on someones driveway. A doctor walked into the cubicle, turning to me, "Lets get a look at you" he said as he shone his torch in my eyes "Are you feeling better young man?" he asked.

"Apart from the sudden blindness from your torch, I feel dandy" I replied faintly.

To which my mum shouted "He's feeling better doctor, I can see that in his sarcasm", as she tapped me on the knee she said "Will you behave".

The doctor pulled a chair to my side and said, "Young man, I have to inform you that you have epilepsy" he said. Just like that - like an off the cuff comment, and I guess if he had tried to put another way it wouldn't have made any difference but he made it sound so matter of fact as if he was telling that my watch had broken or my bike had got a puncture. I looked at my dad (who had tears in his eyes) and then turned and looked at my mum before turning to look at my dad again, "NO, NO, he's got it wrong dad - tell me he has it wrong?" I asked as I felt the tears begin to roll down my face. The horror that hit my body as I was being told that I have the same illness that killed my aunt at the age of fourteen was sending shivers down my spine and for the first time in my life - I was scared, scared of the unknown journey ahead of me from now on.

My dad just shook his head, "It's true son, a teacher from your school saw you on his driveway this morning and you were having an epileptic seizure" he told me as he dropped his head to hide the tears in his eyes.

My mum sobbed "I lost my sister to epilepsy, I am not losing my son as well".

And on that sentence alone (**I lost my sister to epilepsy**) I became horrified and I jumped off the trolley and ran through the accident and emergency department to the sounds of "STOP THAT BOY" being shouted in the distance behind me. I ran through some double doors and found myself on the ambulance bay outside, as I ran in no particular direction, barefoot and in a robe - I found myself running into the hospital carpark and onto the street adjoining before an ambulance stopped and a female paramedic jumped out, "And where do you think you are going wee willy winkie?" she shouted as she grabbed me. "Its a bit cold to be running around in an hospital gown- and no shoes too" she added.

It was the paramedic who had been called out to me previously. By then my dad and the doctor had caught me up and after sitting me inside the back of the ambulance my dad asked, "What the hell do you think you're doing?"

"Running away" I cried as I panted to control my breathing after my sprint, "Running away from who?" Replied my dad.

"Running away from this situation - from epilepsy, if I don't hear what you are telling me then maybe it's not happening, ignorance is bliss" I tearfully explained under my laboured breathing.

"Glyn, you can't run away from this and you can't outrun epilepsy?" explained the doctor,

"Why me?" I cried "Why has this happened to me?"

Turning to the female paramedic I cried "My mums sister died in an epileptic seizure at the age of fourteen - I am fourteen with epilepsy and I don't - I don't … don't want to die" I cried hysterically as my thoughts were focused on the facts that my parents never hidden from us the reasons of aunt Sylvia's death and the young age she was when she died.

The female paramedic hugged me as she tried to console me "You're not going to die" she whispered as my dad interrupted

"I won't let you die son, I will be there all the time for you" he said,

"BE THERE FOR ME, BE THERE FOR ME - I HAVE ALREADY HAD THREE SEIZURES AND YOU WEREN'T THERE FOR ANY OF THEM, NO-ONE WAS THERE, I COULD HAVE DIED IN ANYONE OF THEM..... DIED ALONE" I screamed as I was now beginning to fear that death was a certainty and could be a moment away.

Hugging me tighter the paramedic said, "I'm Michelle but I like my friends to call me Shellie, you can call me Shellie".

"What you saying - FRIENDS?" I asked, (being friends with a pretty woman- in uniform too, seemed good compensation for my plight at the time), "Yes we can be friends but only if you get back in that hospital and accept that you have to let this doctor start the treatment that will see you through this" she added as she wiped away my tears.

"Okay, okay- lets go back but can I have a cup tea when we get back please?" I asked as I reluctantly agreed to go back to the hospital. The ambulance drove us the short distance to the hospital and I walked in with my head hung low in a bid to hide my tears, my tears were my only comfort and my only way of expressing myself at the time - how can you put into words how you feel when you have just been diagnosed with epilepsy?

So now it was official, it had been confirmed by a hospital doctor and a witness on my paper round - I was now an epileptic teenager, a liability to my family and a burden that I have to try to deal with at a time that I was still trying to accept the death of my grandmother.

It was on the doctors advice that we were to keep this news within the family circle because of the stigma and the misunderstanding of epilepsy at that particular time. Many folks have their own opinions of the condition, such as folk bite off their own tongues and are unable to talk again after having an epileptic seizure - each epileptic seizure takes five minutes off your life expectancy and epileptics are capable of killing folk who go near them while they are having a seizure. I know this because my class mates were under this belief of epilepsy when we were discussing the brain in biology a few months previously.

How could this have happened to me, why has this happened to me? I was now facing a future of uncertainty, but how long was my future to be? Next year, next month or next week? How many seizures will I have before one kills me like it did my mum's sister?

I was now repeating to myself my allegations of our new house being cursed and the fact that bad luck comes in three's - well here is the third... epilepsy!

The one fact that epileptics swallow their own tongues and choke to death was what my parents believed to be true and as for me, whether or not it was true - epileptics can die during a seizure and that risk could be greater when asleep. I was scared as I worried that my next seizure would be my last and for a fourteen year old child to be going through this was wrong, totally wrong - wrong for me to be experiencing and wrong for my family to have to witness my seizures and make them feel the kind of pain that was totally unbearable.

I was scared to go to sleep each night because I may have a seizure in my sleep and never wake up again - I may die. And so I would sit up on my bed with my back against the headboard and my head against the wall (with my headphones on, listening to my Queen records) and cry, I would eventually cry myself to sleep and wake up the next morning snug and warm under the duvet - someone had tucked me in bed or I had wiggled under the covers myself? I would wake up the next morning and put my hands together and pray to God "Thank you Lord for giving me another day to live" I would whisper before getting out of bed. I was now missing my grandmother even more, I needed her arms around me and her kiss on my forehead that would signal to me that everything will be okay.

My grandmother used to say that god moves in mysterious ways and that there is a reason for everything in life, but forgive me when I say that I could not find any one reason why any god was now allowing me to have epileptic seizures. My grandmother would see this comment as a kind blasphemy, but I felt this way and questioned 'is there a god and if so - why has he picked on me'? Up to now, I had been a tough kid - I was raised on a council estate whereas you had to learn to fight and stand your ground or run away from bullies, but if you run- you will be running forever. I could face anyone at anytime but now I was reduced to a crying teenager, epilepsy became the bully that anyone would dread to face - a bully that had finally beat me up and would constantly beat me up for a long time to come.

I was now on medication that was prescribed by the hospital and it was a trial and error sort of situation to prescribe mild drugs and then increase the dosage or prescribe something stronger according to my seizures and frequency of the seizures. All was going well and I had not had a seizure for almost two weeks until one Sunday morning, I had woke up and went downstairs with my sister following behind me. "Get the kettle on then" she asked as we walked into the kitchen but as I walked over to the kettle I just stood and stared at my sister, "Glyn, Glyn" she called "are you okay" But I just stared as I heard her scream for my dad - and then everything went black.

I woke up on the kitchen floor with my dad on his knees and leaning over me, my sisters were crying uncontrollably, "Look at my fingers" said my dad as he showed me his hand and the two fingers that had been bitten to the bones. His hand was red with blood and he must of been in great pain (from holding my tongue as I was in a seizure) but he never showed his pain. My mum had telephoned the family doctor who came out as fast as he could, so fast in fact that he knocked our front door in his pyjamas and a dressing gown. After examining me, he told my dad off for putting his fingers in my mouth while I was having a seizure. "Do not under any circumstances put a spoon on his tongue when he has a seizure, do not force your fingers in his mouth - just lie him on his side and his tongue will flop to the side" instructed the doctor, but my dad took no notice as future seizures were to prove whereas I almost bite my dads fingers off completely.

A few days later and I was back at the hospital but this time as an out patient and not an emergency bought in by an ambulance. I was booked for an EEG, I didn't know what an EEG stood for at the time as I thought that EEG made cookers but my mum confirmed that it was ECG who made cookers not EEG, "I have a Belling cooker" interrupted an elderly lady who was sitting next to my mother - which started a conversation about the best manufacturers of cookers between my mum and this lady as I was thinking - "REALLY, COOKERS?". Here I was - about to embark on a the most frightening journey of my life and my mum is sitting in an hospital waiting room talking about ovens, hobs, gas or electric cookers!

I heard my name being called and a nurse walked me into a room with my mum, I was so nervous as I didn't know what to expect, a medic put blobs of gel on different parts of my head and then stuck wires to them.

"I hope he ain't messing my hair up?" I called over to my mum,

"I have a comb in my bag" she replied "Now shut up" she scolded. I asked the medic to explain an EEG and his reply was:-

"An EEG measures electricity that your brain makes. It will determine the type and origin of your seizures. The EEG will show where abnormal activity in your brain comes from and can help distinguish between generalised or focal seizures" he explained.

"You lost me at measures electricity" I thought to myself.

This medic didn't hold back as he told my mum that my EEG readings was completely off the scale and only the strongest of prescribed drugs looked very likely to control my seizures.

After the EEG was an appointment for a CT scan or a cat scan as it was called. A CT scan uses X-rays to obtain cross-sectional images of your brain, CT scans can reveal abnormalities in your brain that might cause a seizure, such as tumours, bleeding and cysts, according to the doctor who was conducting the scan.

I was enjoying this as I lay on a bed and went in and out of a huge round circle - a big donut. This was like space age technology to me and I felt like I was in an episode of Star Trek, "Beam me up Scotty" I called as I was getting off the bed.

"What did you say"? Asked my mum,

"Errm, nothing" I said as I lied to my mum so she didn't have to tell me to behave again. As my dad was at work, we had to catch a bus to and from the hospital and as we sat on the bus home I asked my mum "Aren't you scared that I may have a seizure here - now?"

"Why would I be scared?" replied my mum "No matter where, no matter when you have a seizure - feel safe that I or your father will be keeping you safe". This was reassuring but didn't ease my worries about the possibility of a short lived life span because of epilepsy.

Back at home I was now feeling bored, my older sister had agreed to look after me instead of looking for a job and as this allowed my parents to carry on with their jobs, they paid my sister to look after me. The school holidays were now over and my parents had arranged a meeting with the headmaster of my school who had told them that under no circumstance could he allow me back to school until I got the all clear from the hospital,

"If your son were to have a seizure and fall down any of the staircases, it could be fatal" he told them "If he were to have a seizure while on the way to a lesson, he could be trampled on by hundreds of pupils" he added, "And then there's the stigma of epilepsy, if your son has a seizure at school - he will definitely be the target of bullying from almost every pupil in the school".

The school could not ensure my safety and therefore it would be best if I stayed at home until further notice. And so sitting on my bed listening to my LP's or the radio (day after day) was my only comfort and one day news was being broadcast about the death of Marc Bolan who was killed when his car hit a tree, many T-Rex fans were in mourning for a king of glam rock and many T-Rex songs were being played that day with things going back to normal the following day and the usual chart music was being played once again, but I could only stomach Boney M's 'Ma Baker', Rod Stewart's 'I don't want to talk about it', Paul McCartney and Wings 'Mull of Kintyre', Baccara's 'Yes sir I can boogie' and the likes for so long before putting my Queen LP's on the record player. September the twentieth - Victor the giraffe died for love apparently. Victor, the Amercus giraffe from Marwell zoological park near

Winchester, had spent the night with three lady giraffes and collapsed into the splits and couldn't stand up again. Firemen were called in a bid to try to get him back on his feet but all attempts failed. He had been dosed with drugs to keep his strength up and a frame was built around him in a desperate attempt to hoist him up and back on his feet. It was believed that Victor died from shock. I thought to myself "Bloody hell- fancy dying after a night with three females?"

"What a way to go, myself alone with three women - Farrah Fawcett, Cheryl Ladd and Jaclyn Smith - death by sex with 'Charlie's Angels' (an American TV series), it will be better than dying in a seizure- and a happier way to go.

I tried to be positive, but at this moment of my life I really needed a strong shoulder to cry on - I needed my grandmother and at this point of my life, I was missing her even more. I would have probably stayed at my grandmothers house as I did in the past when I became ill and perhaps the quiet calm atmosphere of her house would have been good therapy for me and as she said her prayers each night before going to bed - I know that she would have prayed for me each and every day.

In a time when there were only three channels on television, no internet, no video recorders, no mobile phones and no computers - it was a bad time to be under house arrest and boy was I going stir crazy or getting cabin fever (whichever way you want to put it). My family were now focusing everything on myself and my illness and it was driving me crazy- it was for my own good but I was getting fed up with my confinement as all I could do was listen to my radio or my records in my bedroom but the final straw (apart from the KENNY ROGERS song 'Lucille' driving me mad) was the song by ANDREW GOLD that was titled 'Lonely boy', the words of "oh what a lonely boy" had summed up my current situation and got me so frustrated - and that frustration would make me throw my radio out of my bedroom window and watch it smash to pieces on the patio below. I had to escape my room and escape from the house, if only for a hour so I could feel fresh air on my face, so I could feel the tarmac beneath my feet and I could have a cigarette without having to hang out of my bedroom window- and yes, I was even risking my life by having a smoke as hanging out of my bedroom window and having a seizure at the same time would certainly kill me. When my grandmothers neighbour told me that smoking will kill me - he didn't mean this way did he? One thing was certain, I needed some freedom and I didn't care at what cost, I wanted to return to the land of the living if only for a few minutes.

Chapter six

The great escape

Now being locked away from the outside world was driving me crazy, yes I had my LP's to listen to - and I would lie on my bed with my headphones listening to Queen all day long, I wish that Freddie Mercury, Brian May, John Deacon and Roger Taylor were to know what comfort they bought me during this bad period of my life and how they had touched the life of a boy that they never even knew.

With most of my family doing their best to cheer me I was having a few surprises bought for me and one day I will never forget, my sister and her boyfriend (now husband) had bought me the new Queen album which was titled 'News of the world' and as I took the LP from its sleeve a few tickets fell from the cover, they had got tickets to see Queen live at Bingley hall in Stafford, I couldn't believe it - Queen live in concert. And though the concert was a few months away my dad refused to let me go.

"No way are you taking him to a venue that will be rammed with people jumping up and down and getting excited" he demanded. "Dad, we will look after him, he'll be okay" pleaded my sister.

"Please dad, please - its Queen live in concert, please let me go" I cried. But my dad was adamant and when he said no, he meant no. I was to see Queen live in many concerts on many occasions in the future but not at this particular moment in time - I was gutted. My dad was rightly concerned about me having a seizure in a packed concert hall and being trampled to death or having a seizure and unable to get medical attention when I need it and I was to admit that he was correct in his assumption and his concerns were valid.

My life was feeling so bad now and I was wondering why on earth am I alive, I didn't want to die at a young age but I was now regretting being born for what was the use of giving me a life and then taking away the right to live it?

The lyrics to Queen songs were now beginning to reflect my feelings and my way of life at the time, with words such as -

"**Sometimes I wish I had never been born at all**" - Bohemian Rhapsody.

"**Each morning I get up I die a little ,Can barely stand on my feet. Take a look in the mirror and I cry, Lord, what you're doing to me**" - Somebody to love.

But the one poignant sentence in any Queen song would be written in 1984 (some seven years later) in the song Radio Ga Ga with the line "**I'd sit alone and watch your light, my only friend through teenage nights**" which would describe my teenage nights as I was confined to my bedroom with just my record player and Queen albums to listen to.

But back in 1977 and by now I was getting angry and upset with the prison that once was a home, I had to break free (no apologies for the Queen pun) and see the outside world - just to feel the air on my skin and feel the sense of freedom if only for an hour or so.

One day I planned my escape and while my sister was in the bathroom I took my dads car keys and jumped in his car - I turned on the radio, I sat in my dads car and lit up a cigarette and I as turned the ignition key - the song 'Red light spells danger' by Billy Ocean came pumping out of the car speakers. With the engine purring away I put the car into gear and slowly drove down the road as my heart started pumping. "Oh my God, I will be in deep trouble if my dad were to see me now" I chuckled to myself as the devil in me was coming out. Thanks to my brother, I knew how to drive a car (in a fashion) but on a field and not on the road and so the excitement was building in me.

I was driving slowly around the estate but I feared driving on any main roads and so I stayed on the estate and slowly drove up and down the same roads as 'Hotel California' by THE EAGLES was playing on the radio. I was enjoying myself totally, "I'M FREE, I'M FREE" I screamed until I spotted my dad standing in the middle of the road and as I bought the car to a shuddery halt, my dad pulled me from the drivers seat and ordered me to sit on the passenger side. I was unaware that my sister had phoned my dad at work to tell him that I had ran away in his car and she was scared that I may have a crash.

We got home and a furious father was reading me the riot act. "What the hell was you thinking?" he shouted, "I was bored" I replied,

"You were bored- bored?" he shouted back. "What if you had a seizure in that car?" he asked. "What if you had a seizure and lost control of the car and driven into innocent pedestrians, killing innocent pedestrians?" my dad asked.

I hadn't thought of that possibility, neither had I got an answer, I had no explanation as to why I acted so irresponsibly - other than I was bored. And this was my life at this moment with the words 'What if you had a seizure' etched in my brain.

"I ought to give you a good hiding" growled my dad.

"Go on then?" I replied,

"WHAT DID YOU SAY?" shouted my dad, "Give me a good hiding, I deserve it" I said.

"What's got into you?" asked my dad as he was now puzzled by my behaviour.

"What's got into me?" I sneered, "A thing called epilepsy has got into me" I cried.

And with the tears beginning to flow, I cried out, "So give me that good hiding, go on - just for once treat me like a normal kid, please just discipline me as you would have if I hadn't got epilepsy" I cried.

"Why are you acting this way?" my dad asked with a puzzled expression,

"I JUST WANT TO BE NORMAL" I screamed in a tear filled rage.

"You are normal" yelled my dad in reply, "WELL IF I AM NORMAL, WHY DO YOU KEEP ME LOCKED AWAY?" I screamed as my tears became heavy. "I don't have time to deal with this" My dad grunted as he stormed out of the house and back to work- taking his car keys with him.

A few weeks later and things were getting back to normal, well normal for my family because being a teenager with epilepsy - life was never normal for me. I would spend days sneaking a look at the photos in my mums biscuit tin, the photos of my aunt Sylvia and I would talk to the picture of a beautiful young girl, "What happens now?" I would ask, "How will this end for me?" I would cry in the hope that a message or a sign would appear as to advise me of my next steps. This was to fuel a notion in my head and so I wanted to visit my aunt Sylvia's grave and I didn't know why, but it was so ironic that the only person who knew what I was experiencing had died before I was born, nevertheless I may find some comfort by visiting my deceased aunt and talking to her headstone and so I was planning to get out and escape.

I went to my record player in my bedroom and put on my new Queen album that was 'News of the world' and I left the arm of the record player in the off position, this meant that the LP would play over and over again and give the impression that I am in my bedroom listening to music - my radio would have been better in this situation as I wouldn't have to worry about the same songs playing over and over again (unless I was tuned into a local radio station). With six tracks on side one of the LP, it would give me around twenty minutes or so before the needle returned to the LP and would start playing all over again. With the thumping intro of 'We will rock you' I made my escape and climbed out of the bedroom window, shimmering down the drainpipe and sneaking my bike from the (new) shed I made good my escape. I felt like Steve McQueen in the film 'The

Great Escape' and that motorbike scene, only I was not planning on jumping any fences on my bike.

Pedalling down the road I realised that I would be facing a dilemma, as I was planning to visit aunt Sylvia's grave I would have to ride past my dad's works and risk him seeing me - so a detour along the canal towpath was the only option available to me. Like a fugitive on the run I cycled my heart out along the towpath and over a small bridge that the locals called the Adam and Eve bridge, along a small back alley and through a cul-de-sac that bought me onto Coltham road and into the cemetery.

I was soon at my aunt's grave and I sat at the foot of the grave and just stared at the headstone that read 'Died, age fourteen years' and then my tears started to roll down my face, "Oh aunt how do I deal with this?" I cried "How long before I end up in my own grave?" I continued as I was convinced that death was the only way to be free from epilepsy. I lit up a cigarette and puffed my way through a tear filled conversation as I knelt down at the foot of a grave.

"I can't go to see Queen in concert because of the risk of a seizure, I'm not supposed to ride my bike because of the risk of a seizure" I said to the grave as my tears began to blur my vision.

"FOR GOD'S SAKE I AM FED UP WITH ALL THIS CRYING, WAS IT LIKE THIS FOR YOU AUNT SYVLIA?" I yelled to the headstone.

"Its no good cursing God" said a voice behind me as I turned to see the local vicar. "Sorry your highness" I replied as I attempted to wipe away my tears.

The vicar chuckled to himself and questioned me of why I wasn't at school and I eventually told him my story and the connection between myself and the aunt who died before I was born. I didn't realise that he had called the authorities to report an absent pupil in his graveyard. The school sent out a truant officer by the name of Miss Wilson, a pretty woman with a nasty attitude who dealt with all the bad kids at all of the schools in our area. Catching children playing truant was her at her best and she revelled in the glory of driving into the school driveway with children she had caught playing truant in the back of her car and making them do the walk of shame to the headmaster's office (I know this from past experience as I too had been caught playing truant).

But as I saw her car parked at the gates of the cemetery I was determined that she wasn't catching me and I jumped on my bike and rode off, cycling on the long grass of the graveyard was slowing me down and I was glancing back at Miss Wilson to see her return to her car and try to cut me off at the 'pass' so to speak. Her plan was to drive to the only possible means of escape for me which was a huge gap in a fence and a dirt path that had been created by walkers over the years, I wasn't going to let her catch me - I couldn't let her catch me. I could feel my heart pumping as I rode across the graveyard, I was huffing and puffing as I forced my legs to cycle faster. As I cycled out of the gap in the fence that led onto a small housing estate I saw to my right the small MG car being driven by Miss Wilson and so I sped up the road and down a small alley that led into the cul-de-sac that had the alley leading to the canal towpath. Speeding down the towpath I spotted the small MG car parked on the brow of Lane head bridge and standing on the towpath beneath was Miss Wilson.

"Does she ever give up" I panted to myself as I turned round and rode off in the opposite direction only to stop briefly to turn around and see her running to her car again. "She will catch me on the roads" I thought to myself "Only one option", I threw my bike over a fence and into someone's garden and then jumped over the fence myself and I did this all along a row of gardens until I reached the end of the row and found myself in a street (did I say that unlike Steve McQueen I wouldn't be jumping any fences?).

"Done it, I have got rid of her" I thought until her small MG car came driving down the street. "Oh God, just go away" I thought as I rode away and eventually into an area of garages behind some of the houses on my estate. But I suddenly realised that this was a dead end with only one way in and out of the garages,

"What will I do, what will I do?" I thought as I looked for an escape. Just then a garden gate opened and a voice shouted, "Over here Glyn, quickly", it was Jane and she ushered me up her garden path and into her house. We went to the upstairs landing window and watched Miss Wilson driving up and down the road, in and out of garage areas looking for her escapee, these houses were built in a compact way and either overlooked each others gardens or overlooked tenants garages - it was easy to see and hear everything that was going on outside. After watching Miss Wilson driving around the estate, we laughed and laughed and eventually went downstairs and into the kitchen.

"So how come you are not at school?" she asked, "You do know that there is a rumour going around the school that you are in a youth offenders prison" she added "You are being called BORSTAL BOY" she laughed.

"How much I want to tell you about myself at the moment but I can't, I am sworn to secrecy" I told her, "Anyway, why aren't you at school?" I asked.

"I got double maths this morning so I faked a migraine" replied Jane "But I have to go to school this afternoon so you will have to go soon" she told me. "So are you going to tell me why you have been avoiding me?" she asked with her arms firmly crossed, "It's been ages since we last met".

So with a sharp intake of breath I plucked up the courage to tell her.

"You have to promise to tell nobody what I am about to tell you" I sighed as I thought I could trust Jane with my secret. She sat and listened to my woeful story of being a victim to epilepsy and how my seizures were changing my life and keeping me a prisoner in my own home. I felt some comfort in actually telling someone about my health, but had I done the right thing? Jane just stared at me as if she were in shock "Right, okay- you have to go" She replied in a stern voice as she stood up "I mean now" she demanded.

"What have I done?" I asked in a shocked manner.

"I don't want a freak in my house" she called, "I ain't no freak" I snapped in defence.

"Glyn, you could have a seizure here and now so just get out or I will call the police" she screamed.

"Call the police - why?" I begged.

"JUST GET OUT OF MY HOUSE" She screamed.

"Okay, I'm going but I will tell you this, you had better not tell anyone at school about me" I shouted at her.

"Oh yeah and what will you do about it if I do?" she smirked.

"Me, I will do nothing but my five sisters may want to have a word with you about it - if you know what I mean" I said.

"Yeah five sisters, errm okay - if you promise not to contact me again, I promise to tell nobody about you, now get out"! she shouted.

And so I walked down the path pushing my bike with my head held low and as I walked from the garden gate into the garages, someone jumped on me.

"GOTCHA" said Miss Wilson as she grabbed me by the arm. "Right, where do you live?" she asked, "Just around the corner" I sighed.

"Great, you can drop your bike off at home and I will take you back to school - oh and you can change into your school uniform too" she told me.

My sister had seen me as I walked towards my front door and was standing in the door way with her arms folded in that 'you're in big trouble' type of stance.

"Where the bloody hell have you been?" she scolded. "You are aware of him playing truant then?" Asked Miss Wilson,

"He's not been playing truant, he's not allowed to go to school - who the hell are you anyway?" Replied my sister.

"I'm the truant officer and I need to see your parents" replied Miss Wilson.

My sister explained that they were at work and she was the responsible adult looking after me until I'm allowed back to school.

"Not doing a very good job of looking after your brother are you?" Scoffed the officer "Allowing him to go out on his bike- on his own" she added.

"I'll deal with you later" whispered my sister as she gave me one of her angry looks.

"Tell your parents that I will see them this evening when they get back from work" Called Miss Wilson as she walked down the path and into her car.

"Mum and dad will go mad when they get home" my sister said, "And you've probably got me in trouble too" she added.

I spent the rest of the afternoon in my bedroom and just lay on my bed waiting for the moment that the front door would open and my parents will walk in. Eventually my parents returned home and Miss Wilson pulled up to our house as they walked through the door, my parents had barely sat down when there was a knock at the door and after exchanging of words with Miss Wilson I was ordered downstairs. We all sat around the table in the dining room and listened to Miss Wilson's version of events and of course my parents were furious.

"What the hell was you doing on your bike?" snapped my dad "And why did you let him go out?" he shouted at my sister.

"I didn't know he had gone out, I was having a shower when he left but afterwards when I went into his bedroom to tell him to turn down his record player- he wasn't there" she explained.

Miss Wilson interrupted by explaining her understanding of my situation. "I have spoken to the head of the school who has informed me that it is not possible to have Glyn back at school at the moment - so I will take steps to get him a place in a boarding school" she told us.

"I ain't going in no boarding school" I yelled as a look of horror crossed my face.

"Too bloody right you're not" snapped my mum.

My dad was now trying to calm my mum as she went into a mad rage, "How dare you walk in here and tell me that you are going to take my son away" shouted my mum.

"It's in his best interest if he goes to a boarding school with staff who are trained to deal with children with special needs" explained Miss Wilson as she was desperately trying to make herself heard over my mums shouting.

"SPECIAL NEEDS?" Shouted my dad "MY SON IS NOT SPECIAL NEEDS" he added.

"Well you can't look after him yourselves can you and he is missing out on his education" she said in her snobbish voice.

"How dare you say that I cannot look after my own children, how dare you" my mum raged as she was standing with her sleeves rolled up. "Get out of my house, get out now" demanded my mum.

Miss Wilson was reluctant to leave until she got my parents to agree to a meeting whereas a decision would be made about my education for the near future.

"I am not asking you - I am bloody telling you, get out of this house now" seethed my mum "You can walk out or be carried out because I am about to knock you on your arse!" And on that Miss Wilson left rather hastily.

My dad stared at me and tutting away he stood up and yelled at me "Look at the trouble you've got yourself into now" said my dad as he wagged his finger in my face, "Why on earth did you go out on your bike, you could have had a seizure in the middle of the road and got yourself run over by a bus or something" he added.

But I quickly responded by saying "I cycled along the canal towpath to avoid the busy roads". To which my mum went mad and in her fit of rage she said "YOU CYCLED ALONG THE CANAL TOWPATH AND RISKED DROWNING? IF YOU HAD A SEIZURE YOU COULD HAVE FELL INTO THE CANAL AND … IT DOESN'T BARE THINKING ABOUT" she cried in horror at the thought of what could have happened.

I hadn't thought of the fact that I could have had a seizure and fallen into the canal. I was asked why I would want to go and visit my aunt's grave and I broke down in tears as I replied, "I needed someone to talk to, someone who understands what I am going through".

"But she's dead, how can you have a conversation with someone who's dead?" Asked my dad. "I just need someone to listen to me, someone who will not try to tell me how I am feeling or how I should spend my time each and everyday" I cried in frustration. "I am bloody fed up with 'what ifs' - what if I had a seizure in this situation and what if I had a seizure in that situation, I need someone to listen to me".

"But you can talk to us, we are your parents and you can talk to us" said my mum who was getting tearful by now.

"I can talk to you till I am blue in the face but you never listen to what I am saying - you just tell me what to do and what not to do" I replied as I stormed out of the room and up the stairs to my bedroom. But what now, what about the possibility of me being sent to a boarding school that could be hundreds of miles away? "OH GOD WHAT HAVE I DONE?" I sighed to myself as I fell down onto my bed.

My dad went into action straight away and took advantage of the many connections he had within the community, he called a local councillor who helped to get our local MP involved and went straight into a plan of action and that plan would mean going to court if need be. The local authorities were very much responsible for my education until my situation could be determined as whether I would fit enough to go to my local school in the near future or if I would need the support of a school equipped and staffed to deal with my health issue. To cut a long paragraph short, it was agreed that I could return to my school if I were fit enough to return before the end of the summer term (end of July 1978) if not, then I would be off to a boarding school - I had just nine months to get over this and between now and July I was to have school work delivered to my house on a regular basis.

Following my escape attempt, my dad had added extra locks to the house and these were mortice locks in addition to the Yale barrel locks that could be opened from the inside by turning a knob and so a key was needed to leave the house (a key I didn't have), he also added security to the window frames which made leaving impossible without a key, I was allowed the key to the window locks of my bedroom only when my parents returned home from work and were able to keep a close eye on me. I was now a prisoner in my own bedroom and my only break from the boredom was the homework bought to me from school, I was getting a visit from a school teacher who would help me with my work for an hour or so. Having Miss Williams visit me for an hour each day was a bonus, all schoolboys had a crush on Miss Williams- myself included. Miss Williams never asked why I was absent from school and I assumed that she knew, which is why I told her one day - she became more supportive after that and promised not to talk about it to anyone (except with my head teacher who was already aware of the situation). At this point I should point out that Katie (Kitty) had agreed to take over my paper round until I was well enough to go back to work and being the sister she was, she shared some of the wages each week so I could have enough money to buy some cigarettes (that she would get for me as I wasn't allowed to go to the shops).

I was now missing school and in despair when listening to my sisters stories of what had been happening at school, I was now in a state of mind that made me more argumentative and I would disagree with all of my family over any issue so I could cause an argument. I called it being constantly bored but my parents called it attention seeking and told me off more and more about it.

Things came to boiling point when my dad announced that a day trip to Blackpool had been planned by the 'King Charles in the oak' pub darts team for their families as a thank you to the mothers and children for putting up with the fact that the team had been going to the Jollies night club in Stoke on Trent almost every evening for the previous week to watch a darts tournament (my dad loved darts and was a fan of Eric Bristow, John Lowe and Jocky Wilson). All children were invited except for me because a crowded place like Blackpool during the illuminations was not a safe place for a kid with epilepsy. This was the final straw and I was not accepting this decision by my parents, I pleaded my case to my parents time and time again until they agreed to think it over. Eventually I was allowed to go but only if I agreed to stay close to my mum and not to go on any roller coaster rides or any ride that could be a danger to a child who may have a seizure during any particular ride, I agreed to anything they asked as I was desperate to get a spot of leave from my prison - sorry, my home.

Chapter seven

Dicing with death?

I couldn't wait to go to Blackpool and I was so excited, usually I wouldn't be this excited about a day trip to anywhere but a chance to get out of the house for a whole day was so inviting. I will be miles and miles up north which meant miles and miles away from the whole epilepsy scenario and the prison inmate environment that my parents were forced to put on me for my own safety. We were picked up by a coach outside the King Charles pub and off toward the M6 motorway, even the view of fields and the odd factory from the window of the coach was a delight to my eyes as I was taking in every bit of scenery I could on the journey.

When we arrived in Blackpool we were told the plan for the day, a walk around the shops before meeting up at the pleasure beach at late afternoon for a ride on the roller coasters - then the coach will drive through the illuminations before heading for the motorway, we will be back at the pub for around ten thirty in the evening.

Blackpool is a busy place and this day was no different as many people were pushing their way through crowds of people walking in the opposite direction to them, this caused my mum to try to hold my hand to keep me safe but I kept pushing her hand away "I'm too old to be holding my mummy's hand" I sarcastically shouted over the noise of the crowded sea front. Eventually I was offered a hand to hold by a young lady named Liz, "Here, take my hand handsome" she said as I grabbed her hand straight away. "I'll keep him safe Eileen" she called to mum as we swung our hands together and acted like silly little children to the annoyance of my mum. I taught Liz the lyrics to 'seaside rendezvous' a track from the 'Night at the opera' album by Queen and for a while we were both singing "Seaside, whenever you stroll along with me …" again this was beginning to annoy my mum and I think it was because an older woman holding a teenagers hand and acting childish may have been seen as inappropriate.

Liz held onto me all day and the thrill of walking hand in hand with a beautiful woman was now wearing off toward the afternoon and I was getting really fed up with having a chaperone or a bodyguard with me all day long. As we made our way to the pleasure beach complex I looked in excitement at the rides and roller coasters that were shooting around the park. "Don't get any ideas of going on any of these rides" my mum ordered, "You are keeping your feet firmly on the ground"!

In 1977 the pleasure beach rides were pay on entry and not the tickets or wristbands that they use in modern days and so I had saved some of my money for the evening as I intended on going on at least one ride and the one ride I was planning on riding was the 'Grand national' roller coaster ride which is an old wooden construction and the sound of the train like thudding on the ride is a thrill within itself. I loved this ride and any visit to Blackpool was not complete unless I had rode the Grand national, in the past I had been on almost every ride and roller coaster on the complex - and though I had promised to resist the temptation of sneaking on a ride, I was always intent on going on the Grand national.

But my embarrassment started as I was allowed to go on the river caves ride with Liz, the river caves is a very slow boat ride along a makeshift river and through many caves that resemble ancient Egypt, Greece, Garden of Eden and Aztec.

"Ooh its like riding through a tunnel of love" shouted Liz in excitement as if she were on a white knuckle ride, she may have been trying to make this ride seem more enjoyable than it actually was to get me in a happier mood - it didn't work though. This ride was a long and slow journey through many different parts of the world and really is a nice ride, but for a thrill seeker it is no substitute for a fast and winding roller coaster.

The end of the ride was a short drop down a pretend waterfall - a conveyor belt that takes you back to the start and on this drop was a viewing platform were folk would be watching the ride, I cringed in embarrassment as most of the members of our party was looking at me and giggling. As we walked out of the ride my mum was waiting to meet us. "Did you enjoy that son" she asked in delight "See, there are a few rides you can go on" she joyfully added.

I was getting really annoyed by now and that annoyance was made worse by the fact that my sisters and the other kids in our party were going on every ride in the complex (having to go so long without a cigarette didn't help) but I was abiding my time, I was just waiting for the exact moment to make my escape to freedom, well the grand national ride. The atmosphere of the pleasure beach was exhilarating as different sounds screamed out aloud as you walked around the complex, the sounds of ghostly screams from the haunted house were accompanied by the music from other rides that were also accompanied by the sounds of carriages racing around the tracks of rides such as the big dipper.

As I walked around with my mum and other parents in our group I asked my mum if I could find the toilets and I will be back in a few minutes, "You must of have thought I was born yesterday" she laughed sarcastically, "As soon as you are out of sight, you will jump on a ride" she went on to say.

Well that was my plan thwarted but then my mum said, "Actually I need the loo" and after asking some of our party to keep an eye on me, she walked toward the toilets.

I waited for my mum to go out of view "I will catch my mum up" I shouted to the party as I walked away but instead of joining the queue for the toilets, I joined the queue for the grand national ride and as I stood there my heart was beating at a tremendous rate with the excitement of actually going on the ride and the thought that my mum will find out where I have been added to the thrill.

I was so delighted to be sitting securely in the front carriage of the ride and the excitement was greater as we were being pulled to the top of the peak of this huge ride by the sound of a huge chain clanking away, reaching the peak of the roller coaster was signalled with a sign that read 'THEY'RE OFF' and in grand national style there are two separate carriages on two separate tracks that go up and down huge drops as they race each other and with each drop and climb representing a fence on the grand national. I screamed in complete excitement as we were thrusted around the ride, up and down huge climbs and around sharp bends were to add to the thrill of the ride - I held my arms in the air and screamed "LOOK, NO HANDS" as I dared to sit in the carriage without holding on and for the time I was to be on the ride I was free, I was in another world and in another dimension where epilepsy was unheard of and seizures were banned. At that moment in time, if that ride was the last thing I had done before I died - I would have died the happiest boy in the world for it was a taste of how my life used to be, my life before epilepsy. As the carriage came down the final drop, I could see my mum with the crowd from our party and they were all pointing towards the ride (a sign that I had been spotted).

After the ride had ended I was walking from the ride and toward the area where I last saw my group, and they were there waiting for me with my mum in the middle of the group with her arms folded in that angry stance that mums adopt when they are angry with their kids. My mum walked toward me, "What the bloody hell have you been up to" she shouted, "I've been on that ride" I replied as I pointed toward the grand national. "What was you told about roller coasters, you agreed to stay off them" she yelled.

"I forgot" I sneeringly replied.

"FORGOT, MY ASS" she yelled again.

By now I was getting really annoyed, "What is the problem?" I asked my agitated mother.

"The problem is - you could have had a seizure up there and fallen to your death" cried my mum who now in tears at thought that her son could have been killed.

"But I didn't fall to my death, I am very much alive" I replied sarcastically.

"Don't you dare take that attitude with me" she snapped, "Is a ride on a roller coaster worth risking your life for?" Asked my mum.

"MY LIFE, MY LIFE?" I screamed as I burst into floods of tears, "I HAVE NO BLOODY LIFE, I CAN'T TAKE A SHOWER BECAUSE I MAY HAVE A SEIZURE AND SUFFER A FATAL BLOW TO MY HEAD AS I FALL, I CAN'T HAVE A BATH WITHOUT LEAVING THE BATHROOM DOOR OPEN SO EVERYONE CAN SEE THAT I AM OKAY, I CAN'T RIDE MY BIKE, I CAN'T GO SWIMMING AND I CAN'T BE TRUSTED NEAR THE KETTLE IN CASE I HAVE A SEIZURE AND SCALD MYSELF - SO YOU TELL ME WHAT LIFE DO I HAVE AND IS IT REALLY WORTH LIVING?" I cried hysterically as a crowd of nosey onlookers started to form around.

"YOU UNGRATEFUL LITTLE SOD" shouted my mum, "THE WHOLE FAMILY ARE WALKING ON EGG SHELLS SO THEY DON'T SAY THE WRONG THING TO UPSET YOU, WE ARE ALL LIVING OUR LIVES TO MAKE YOURS AS COMFORTABLE AS CAN BE"! She shouted.

"YEAH - IS THAT TRUE?" I yelled as the sting of my tears were hurting my eyes "LET ME TELL YOU ONE THING, I WISH I HAD DIED UP THERE ON THAT RIDE BECAUSE I HAVE NOTHING WORTH LIVING FOR - NOTHING" I screamed "I WISH I WAS DEAD" I cried in floods of tears as I fell to my knees.

My mum went down on her knees next to me and put her arms around me, pulling me to her chest she cried, "I lost a part of me when my sister died in a seizure", To which I wrongly interrupted with, "And wasn't she the lucky one to be given a way out from epilepsy".

My mum then quickly stood up and pulled me to my feet with her, "LUCKY- YOU THINK SHE WAS LUCKY?" Screamed my mum who had now got hold of me by the shoulders of my coat, "SHE WAS SUFFERING THE SAME AS YOU BUT SHE DIDN'T GO AROUND FEELING SORRY FOR HERSELF ALL THE TIME - SHE KNEW SHE HAD EVERYTHING TO LIVE FOR" she continued "EVERYTHING TO LIVE FOR BUT WASN'T GIVEN THE CHANCE TO LIVE HER LIFE". She sobbed.

"BUT HAVING EPILEPSY MEANS HAVING NO LIFE, I CANNOT DO ANYTHING FOR FEAR OF …. OH WHAT'S THE POINT?" I cried as I stared at my mother.

Then as my mum started to wipe away my tears she gently whispered, "Sixteen years ago I lost my sister to epilepsy and I have just learned to live with the loss and living with that loss isn't easy - if I were to lose anyone of my kids, I would never get over it.. I would die myself if you were to die my son" And as her tears flowed uncontrollably she cried "I don't want to lose you - I am never going to lose you".

I started to cry all over again as my mum went on to say, "It tears me apart when I see you in a seizure on the floor and shaking violently, I want to hold you but I can't, I want to put my hands inside your head and remove the thing- whatever it is that makes you have seizures, but I can't, I just have to watch and cry" she told me as she weeped on my shoulder "It hurts, it hurts to see you in a seizure my son so please don't think that you are suffering alone" she cried "Don't ever think that you are suffering alone".

I cried even more as my mum and I hugged each other tightly, for myself having epilepsy meant that I would experience a change in my life but for my parents it was as if history was repeating itself - part of that history being a death in the family because of epilepsy. My parents never showed it but the fear of losing their son during a seizure was on the forefront of their minds and I will admit to sharing their fears, I was scared of having to face what was ahead of me - I was petrified and my attitude was to live what is left of my life doing what I want (if allowed).

The coach journey home was with an awkward atmosphere, the folk who were previously unaware of my condition were now aware that I have epilepsy- my secret was out. I sat alone toward the rear of the coach as I had the feeling that folk were staying out of my way, could it be that they wanted to leave me alone because I was so upset or because they fear a boy with epilepsy (I think it was the latter). Eventually Liz came and sat with me and she cuddled me until I fell asleep and the fear of falling asleep was no longer a feeling I had as I couldn't be bothered about dying in my sleep - not waking up from a sleep would be a good way to go, a painless way to go, and boy was I in a frame of mind where I would be welcoming death as a blessing.

The air brakes of the coach was to wake me up as we pulled outside the King Charles pub, I woke up with my head on Liz's lap and the sight of her knees were the first thing I saw but in my sleepy state (and my head lying to one side) I was to wonder where I was - I couldn't make out what a pair of women's legs were until I sat up. Liz kissed me on the cheek before saying goodbye and driving away in her car.

By now my mouth was dry and I was in need of a drink and as I walked into the bar room of the pub I saw my dad playing cards with his mates at a table, "Dad I need a drink" I called as I walked up to his table. Now the tables in this pub were all old fashion tables with solid cast iron legs that had patterns and heads of lions on them. "Dad, can I have a drink please?" I asked but as my dad stood up to get me a drink - everything went black.

I woke up on the settee at home with my family around me, my dads fingers were oozing blood and my mum was crying hysterically along with one of my sisters (Yasmin), it was the first time that Yasmin had seen me in a seizure and it was the worse thing she had witnessed in her life - made worse by the fact that it was her younger brother having the episode. My dad ignored advice to go to the local hospital to get stitches in his fingers and wrapped bandages around them instead.

"Just over three hours ago he was on a roller coaster" my mum cried "He sneaked off and went on a roller coaster" she told my dad.

My dad looked at me and said "Dicing with death?" he went on and asked "Why are you so determined to act so bloody irresponsible?" "You could have easily had 'this' seizure at the top of that ride and instead of lying on the settee - you'd be lying on a slab in a hospital morgue - you bloody idiot" he shouted at me with tears in his eyes.

I couldn't reply as my body and my mind was numb and I watched my mum put an ice cold cloth to my forehead to nurse the swelling to my head. When I fell in my seizure at the pub I hit my head on the cast iron leg of the table that my dad was sitting at, I was to have the imprint of the lions head on my forehead for many weeks to come. However, the biggest hurt was that everyone in the pub had witnessed my seizure and this included some children who attended my school and therefore I was not looking forward to my eventual return to school (whenever that may be). When my body returned to planet earth, my way of explaining when my body had returned to normal after a seizure - I sat on the edge of my bed and I couldn't believe the risk that I had taken in Blackpool, for I was destined to have a seizure that day and that seizure could have been at anytime. There were never any signs, no way of knowing when a seizure would happen, no routine of which to time the seizures - they came when they bloody felt like it and floored me each time. It was like being in a boxing ring with an invisible man, not knowing when the next blow was coming and not knowing what direction it was coming from - epilepsy would sneak up on me and take over my body each time.

My appointment at the hospital was now bought forward as requested by the family doctor and new drugs were needed to be prescribed to control my seizures (even though I thought that there was no help for me). After witnessing my seizure in the pub, a school friend came to my house and was I surprised to have a visitor who was a little older than myself. We sat in the dining room and talked about what I was missing at school and then the conversation turned to the episode in the pub after the Blackpool trip.

"So what's happened to you mate?" Asked Simon "You were so bloody stupid to ride alone on a roller coaster in your condition" he added.

"I don't know what's happening to me mate, I really don't know - one day I woke up in the middle of a cul-de-sac and my life hasn't been the same since" I explained "The grand national ride seemed a good idea at the time but looking back I had put myself within a few hours of death - I didn't think about any seizures that day, I just didn't care to be honest" I sighed.

"I am supposed to keep it a secret, especially from school" I explained "There's a stigma around epilepsy and folk may ridicule me".

Then to my surprise Simon stated that he had made the other children who witnessed my seizure promise to say nothing at school - or else they would have him to deal with.

"And if anyone at school does get to find out, I will make sure that they do not make fun of you mate" he said.

I was now wondering why this hard tough nut of a kid is willing to defend me, why has he taken the time to visit me and see how I am- what is his motive? Simon was to tell me that his younger brother (who was in the same year as me at my school) was suffering epilepsy and though his seizures were not as severe and violent as the one he witnessed me having in the pub, it was still heartbreaking to see his brother go through the episodes that he has to endure. This was the first time that I realised that I was not the only person in the world to have epilepsy and because folk were encouraged to keep quiet about the illness, there would be little chance of talking to anyone who would be suffering from epilepsy.

Perhaps one day in the future, epilepsy will not have the stigma it has today and folk will be able to talk about it without fear of ridicule - maybe folk will understand the condition and not fear the word epilepsy, let's hope it will happen one day.

Chapter Eight

Solitary confinement

My exile away from the outside world was to protect me from harm and the fact that the outside world could be a very hostile environment to a boy with epilepsy but what my confinement could not protect me against was the rumours that were now rife about my health following the seizure in the King Charles pub.

My sister Kate would come home from school and cry that some kids had been teasing her about my epilepsy with cruel jokes about the condition, I told her to see Simon and he would sort the situation out at school. But it wasn't kids at my school who were making fun, it was kids at a neighbouring school who lived on our estate who were teasing her. Kate had offered to deliver my newspapers for as long as she was needed to, and because she used to help me in the past- she knew the round quite well. As she had to deliver newspapers in Furzebank way she would have to pass the comprehensive school that was just up the road from where we lived and where some of our neighbours sent their children.

I was furious and so angry that folk who called themselves friends to your face would be so nasty behind your back and so I planned to confront these so called friends about their treatment toward my sister. One afternoon I sat on my garden wall and waited for the stream of kids that would be walking home from school until I spotted the one of the culprits that were named by Kate.

"Hi mate" shouted Paul as he walked toward me, "How are you" he continued as he came near to me,

I punched him full in the face and as his nose exploded with blood I shouted, "I FEEL A LOT BETTER NOW", "How dare you pick on my sister- how dare you" I yelled as Paul lay on the ground. "We were just joking Glyn" said one of his mates, "We didn't mean nothing by it". "You are obviously having a seizure" said Paul as he got to his feet. "I am what?" I asked.

"I want it to be known that Glyn put me on my ass only because I was attacked while he was having a fit- otherwise I would have beaten him up" shouted Paul to his mates.

"Dogs have fits, people have seizures you ignorant sod" I yelled as I squared up to Paul and was ready to unleash another punch. By now my sister (Denise) had come out to see what was going on and eventually got me to go back in the house, and as she followed me into the house. "What do I do now?" I asked my sister as I realised that I had just made a bad situation even worse.

"Nothing you can do" she replied "Just hope that they will forget over time" she added. "Why should I hope that they will forget, they should be sympathetic - understanding" I cried in anger.

"You can't expect anyone to be sympathetic to a condition that they don't understand" explained my sister. "Folk have many misunderstandings about epilepsy and some folk fear those who are suffering from it" she added.

"Have you told your boyfriend that I have epilepsy?" I asked. "Why should I tell him?" she replied. "Have you told him?" I asked again. "No, No I haven't" my sister replied "But only because it's none of his business"! "Or because you are too ashamed to tell him" I snapped back as I ran upstairs to the sanctuary of my bedroom. A few hours later I was called downstairs to talk to a visitor - that visitor being Jane, Jane just stared at me as I walked down the stairs and with her eyes welling up she softly asked "How are you feeling?"

I just shook my head and replied "God knows how I am feeling, I'm so confused at the moment" I sighed as I sat on the steps at the bottom of the stairs.

Jane sat next to me and held my hand and with tears in her eyes she told me with her voice barely in a whisper "I was there in the pub with my parents when you had your seizure, I didn't realise - I didn't know that it affected you in that way" she went on to say as her tears got heavier "I thought epilepsy was about folk going into a fit of uncontrollable rage who would lash out at anyone nearby, I didn't realise that it could so cruelly take over someones body as it did you".

Jane stared at me for a while before asking "How did you get it - is it hereditary?" I replied "My mum's sister had epilepsy when she was young but I don't think it's passed on - it's just one of those things that happen to some folk I guess".

"Your mum's sister, is she free from seizures now?" Jane asked.

"Yes she is free - she died at the age of fourteen, in a seizure" I sighed in reply.

Jane looked horrified as she replied "You are fourteen, you're not going to die are you?"

"Hopefully not, but at this moment in time - I couldn't care less if I live or die" I replied as I hung my head and watched my tears fall from my face and onto my knees. "Do you know that one day I woke up in a cul-de-sac, I didn't know how I got there but as I opened my eyes I could see my bike and my newspapers but I didn't recognise that they were mine. I have racked my brain over and over again but I still cannot remember waking up that day, I cannot remember collecting my newspapers and I can't recall anything about that day before I woke up in that cul-de-sac" I added.

"Do you think that banging your head when you fell off your bike may be the reason that you are having seizures?" Jane asked.

"No, it is likely that I went into a seizure before coming off my bike - the seizure caused the fall and I was probably out cold before I hit the ground" I explained.

Jane kissed me softly on the cheek and wiped away a few of my tears "I am sorry for the way I treated you that day" she sighed, "Oh yes - when you kicked me out of your house" I replied with a frown.

"That was so bad of me and I am sorry, please forgive me" Jane sighed.

But the truth is I would have forgiven her anything as I needed as many friends as possible at this moment in my life and Jane would be a friend, not a girlfriend in the sense of 'going out' together - just a friend. As Jane left my house she promised that she would come round to see me now and then but I told her not to worry for I am used to being home alone without friends for company, I have now accepted my solitary confinement. A huge part of my confinement was following the news on television and a story that had dominated the year, on the tenth of October missing 20-year-old prostitute Jean Jordan was found dead in Chorlton near Manchester nine days after she was last seen alive. Police believe that the Yorkshire ripper may have killed her; the first crime outside of the Yorkshire area which the killer has been suspected of. Also was the story of Christine Eadie and Helen Scott whom were both aged seventeen and disappeared after leaving the World's End pub in Edinburgh, Scotland. Their bodies were found tied and strangled in the countryside the next day. It would be in the year 2014 that serial killer Angus Sinclair was to be convicted of the crime. I followed these stories and to be honest the thought of victims being violently murdered was to make my situation feel less significant in comparison to what those victims families were going through.

By now the gang on the estate of which I was once a part of had now turned against me because of my almost breaking Paul's nose (though I felt that their opinion of me having epilepsy was a part of it too) and as I would sit on my window sill and have a cigarette with the window open I would get a group of kids in the street below shouting, "Don't have a fit and fall to your death", called someone.

"My mums looking for someone to lay her carpet - and you're the only **fitter** I know around here", laughed another (referencing epileptic 'fits').

I just looked at them and shouted,"I will get my own back, just wait and see - I will get each and everyone of you, you'll see".

And then I would close my window, lie on my bed and cry. Life was so unfair, have I done anything so bad that I was being punished in this way? Epilepsy was a condition that I had been aware of all my life because of my mum's stories about her younger sister but even though I practically grew up with these stories, I wondered as to why I still had little understanding of the condition - was it because admitting to having epilepsy was taboo and folk were afraid to admit to having the condition due to the stigma? Even though I was reminded that there were other folk who were suffering epilepsy and I was not alone in this situation - I would never get to talk to anyone else in my area about epilepsy because no-one would be brave enough to admit to having the condition, and boy did I feel all alone, so alone. Maybe one day in the future epilepsy will not be feared as it is today and folk can talk about the condition without fear of a backlash of discrimination bore from ignorance - I need that day now!

The gang on my estate were now making a two to three times a week routine to stand beneath my bedroom window and shout abuse that would have an 'epilepsy' theme. I would endure shouts of "Kidderminster carpets are looking for an experienced fitter", fitter as in epileptic fits. They would shout out, "Glyn, we are starting up a punk rock band and we have Craig who will be 'Victor Vomit', Paul will be 'Peter Puke' and you Glyn can be **Epilepsy Eric**" someone would shout, to which my dad would run out into the street and confront the kids outside of our house who would run away. I would quickly close my bedroom window and hide behind my curtains until my dad had gone back into the house, only to open my window so I could finish my cigarette. I was not allowed out of the house but thankfully my sister Kate would sneak a packet of cigarettes to me now an then, Kate is eleven months younger than me - her real name is Caroline but she prefers to be called Kate, I call her Kitty and I am the only one allowed to call her by that name. Having a sister born so close to when I was born was to forge a bound between us - oh we had our rows and our fights, well I say fights but in reality Kate would knock the crap out of me before my epilepsy.

Over the weeks my tears of self pity was now turning to anger and a rage was rising within me, it was bad enough fighting the condition that had limited my life but to fight everyone who didn't understand epilepsy was a challenge I didn't want to take on, but one I would have to try and conquer if I were ever allowed to go back to a normal life. And I was a normal kid, the same Glyn Marston that I had always been but some kids were treating me as an alien, a wild animal that should be avoided at all costs - this was so unfair and so depressing.

But my exile from the group of kids on our estate was soon to come to an end, as one evening I was in my bedroom and I could hear a lot of shouting in the street below. I was feeling a little scared as my parents were out at the pub (I think my dad had a darts tournament that he was playing in), my sister was in the bathroom - she seemed to spend a lot of time in the bathroom, she spent so much time in front of a mirror that at one point I thought she had a twin sister.

I slowly peered out of my bedroom window to see the group of kids who had been making fun of me for having epilepsy being chased by a gang from another estate. This group of only four kids had ran into the garages behind my house and were hiding from the gang who greatly outnumbered them and were now closing in on them. So I ran downstairs and out to the garden gate - I opened it to see four of my so-called mates cowering in a corner of the garages.

"In here- NOW" I shouted as I urged them to run into my garden.

"No way, we don't need your help" shouted Mickey,

"You have nowhere to hide, so get in here now" I called to the group.

Each one thanked me as they reluctantly stepped through the patio doors and into the living room. "What's that about" I asked as we walked into our kitchen.

"I have been seeing a girl on the Beach-dale estate and I didn't know that she had another boyfriend" replied Paul who was still sporting bruising around the eyes from the day I punched him in the face.

"Yes, that boyfriend and his gang have chased us all the way from the Beach-dale estate and all the way along Bentley lane" said Craig, "Oh by the way - I am sorry for that carpet fitter joke the other night".

"I ain't sorry about what I said" muttered Mickey,

"Well you can leave this house then mate and let the Beach-dale gang do my dirty work for me and give you the good hiding you deserve" I shouted as I ushered Mickey to the front door.

"Okay, okay - I am sorry for what I said the other night" shouted Mickey as he pleaded for me to let him stay in the safety of my house.

We all went up into my bedroom because we could a good view of Bentley lane and that view was all the way to the bridge that went over the M6 motorway near junction ten, we decided to sit there and wait until we could see the gang walking back home to their own estate and then my friends would know it was safe to leave the house and go home.

Looking at the posters on my bedroom walls and the records by my record player, "I didn't know that you were a fan of Queen" said Paul,

"I have been for a few years now" I replied, "So am I, what's you favourite track on any album"? Asked Paul,

"How can you choose a favourite track on any Queen album?" I asked, "Yes, it's difficult to choose but Love of my life is a good track" said Paul,

"What about we will rock you" shouted Craig as he started to stomp his feet on my bedroom floor.

At that point I put on the 'We will rock you' record and we all clapped and stamped in time with the beat and sang out "WE WILL, WE WILL ROCK YOU".

My sister came into the room to see what was going on but quickly went out again and just left us to it as we listened and sang to almost every track of my Queen LP's. But it was clear that this group had to leave my house before my parents returned home and looking from my bedroom window to see if it was safe for my 'mates' to leave was met with a great relief as we spotted the gang from the Beach-Dale estate walking up Bentley lane and back home.

"Thanks for bailing us out mate" said Paul as he stood outside my front door, "Look, I apologise for picking on your sister - I'm sorry for the other night outside your bedroom window and I am sorry that you have been struck down with fits" said Paul in a soft and sympathetic voice.

"Mate, dogs have fits and I have seizures" I sighed "But that said, apology accepted" I laughed, "Look lads, I am still the same kid you have always known - I haven't changed in any way and I am still me, the me that I have always been" I explained.

"Being confined to the house is my parents way of protecting me from.. from" I tried to explain, "From idiots like us who don't understand?" Interrupted Paul. "Something like that" I laughed.

"I have been confined to my own house but now that my secret is out, I have no point in hiding away" I explained to a group of kids who were intimidating me a few days previously.

'You don't have to hide away mate" said Mickey "Friends are friends no matter what".

"Glyn, why don't you ask your parents if you can have friends visit you - if you can't leave the house then why we can't we spend some time with you in your house?" Asked Craig.

And it was a great idea, why should I lose touch with my friends because I have to be confined to the house? If I can't go out to hang around with my mates then they can come here and I am sure my parents will agree to it.

And my parents agreed to having friends in the house, it was great to be back in touch with human life and I felt that my life was going back to normal. This feeling of happiness was extended by the fact that my parents would go to the Bridge pub on Lane Head bridge and this pub had a small family room, I was allowed to go with my parents to the pub and my mates would be there too. We would put all of our loose change into the jukebox and select 'We will rock you' and 'We are the champions' by Queen and we would belt out these songs in the family room.

It was great to actually get of the house and see more than the four walls of my bedroom, I felt part of the gang again but more importantly, I felt part of the human race again - I was happy, really happy.

However, one evening in the Bridge pub and while my friends and I were all singing "WE WILL ROCK YOU" to the music coming from the jukebox - everything went black …. and I woke up at home on the settee.

"Look at my fingers" called my dad as he showed me the blood dripping from his hand.

My eyes were yet again scanning the room and I could see Paul and Craig in the living room who were crying their eyes out, apparently they insisted on coming back to my house to make sure that I was going to be okay. "We didn't do anything- honestly, we didn't do anything" cried Paul, "It's okay, it's okay" replied my mum as she invited the two friends to sit down.

"Are you feeling better Glyn?" called Craig.

But my parents informed them that it would take a while for me to come round and be responsive. "It's best that you go home now but you can pop round in the morning if you like" requested my mum.

Paul and Craig left, and I am guessing that they had tears in their eyes all the way home looking at how upset they were.

Chapter nine

Back to reality

The following day I managed to walk downstairs and into the kitchen (my parents had put me to bed the previous evening as they always did following a seizure), my mum ushered me into the living room and sat me on the settee.

As she packed cushions around me for some kind of protection I mumbled, "Is this really necessary?" As I looked around me and felt like a baby in a crib.

Before she could answer me there was a knock at the front door, my mum answered the door to Paul and Craig and as they walked into the living room they burst into tears as they looked at me and the bruises on my face following the fall from the previous evenings seizure. "I have never seen anything like it in my life" cried Paul "And I don't want to see anything like it again- ever"! he added.

"It was horrible to witness" cried Craig "You are so bloody brave to go through that" added Craig as he was referring to my seizures.

"I am the only one who knows nothing about the seizures mate" I explained "I have no idea of what is happening, no feelings and emotions" I went on to explain. "The real horrible part is when I come round from a seizure and I can see what is happening around me but I can't respond, I can't talk and I can't move a limb - it's like being paralysed for a while" I explained to the two upset friends.

They were really shocked to see someone in an epileptic seizure and were hoping never to witness it again.

"Mickey was so upset that he puked up in the toilets" said Paul,

"He threw up all over the walls, the cistern and the toilet seat, there was vomit everywhere" added Craig.

We sat there for a few hours and discussed epilepsy and the cause of seizures and though my friends were asking a lot of questions, I couldn't give them an answer as to why I had been struck down with this illness. "I feel so ashamed about the jokes I had made about you in the past" sighed Paul.

"How can this happen to a fit kid like you?" Craig asked "I mean - you are the only person I know who has swam from the Adam and Eve bridge to Lane Head bridge" Craig added.

"I remember that day, it was the easiest pack of Benson and hedges that I had earned - a pack of twenty if I could swim in the canal between the two bridges" I laughed. "Mind you my dad was angry when he found out".

"I am sorry for the abuse" Paul added once again.

"Yes, I have no pride in admitting to shouting abuse too mate" added Craig as he made reference to the epilepsy jokes that he had called up to my bedroom window. "I am so sorry" he added.

But I had to be the bigger person in this situation and harbouring thoughts of resentment would not be of any advantage to me at this particular time, I needed to stay friends with as many folk as possible and to try to make those friends be more understanding of my condition - erase their fears and misunderstandings of epilepsy.

"It's hard to see you like this mate" Paul sighed "Is there a cure?" he asked.

"No cure I'm afraid, I just have to hope that I get the medication to control my seizures" I replied "Death is the only way to free me from these seizures".

"You're not going to die - are you?" Craig asked.

"My mum's sister died in a seizure and she too was fourteen years old at the time" I explained.

"Are you scared - scared that you may die in a seizure?" Asked Paul.

"I fear death but if death was the only way to be free of these seizures - I'd choose death any day" I responded with tears rolling down my face, "I am fed up with the bruises, fed up with the limitations on my life, fed up with biting my dads fingers to the bones and fed with the heartache that this is causing my family" I added.

"You're not going to kill yourself are you?" Craig asked.

"No, I am not suicidal but the fear of dying in a seizure no longer worries me and if one day everything went black and I never recovered from a seizure - I would have gone peacefully and without any pain" I added as I tried in vain to stop the tears rolling down my cheeks.

A few weeks later (as before) my hospital appointment was bought forward in a bid to try me with new medication (as the previous medication had failed me) and after a few months of taking phenobarbitone tablets, I was to try something else in the hope that it will be the miracle cure I need - well cure is the wrong word, I would never be cured but anything to control the seizures and keep them at bay would be welcoming.

Phenobarbitone is a suppressant that had been proven to control generalised seizures, but it hadn't been effective in controlling my seizures and so I was to try something new. I was to be prescribed Phenytoin and though I thought it was a new drug, it was first produced in 1936- in Germany I think. I was happy to be trying something (apparently) new and was keeping my fingers crossed that this would be the drug to give me back my independence - but I could only hope.

By now I was back to being confined to my house and though I was allowed visitors, the visits were becoming less and less as my friends were looking forward to seeing their girlfriends more than visiting me, my mates were more interested in sitting in the family room of the pub with their girlfriends than sitting with me and talking about the day I would be free from seizures.

On December the 8th, my parents wanted to celebrate not only my fifteenth birthday but a whole year since we moved into the new house in Farmhouse road- I was not so enthusiastic about celebrating the house move, as I still thought it was cursed - the house of the damned, well it was damned for me. Okay, it was a new build house and we were the first to live in it but what if it had been built on an old graveyard as in the film 'Poltergeist' and I am the one chosen to pay the price for builders and developers who moved the headstones as to make it look like the graves had been totally removed to another area? These thoughts were totally stupid but were dominating my reasons for the run of bad luck that my family had been experiencing over the past twelve months and so I looked for anything to take my mind from anything that may be epilepsy related. And so in the news - Fourteenth of December, a twenty five year old prostitute by the name of Marilyn Moore, was injured in an attack believed to have been committed by the Yorkshire ripper and despite numerous appeals by the police, the Yorkshire ripper still evaded capture. Twenty first of December, four children died at a house fire in Wednesbury, West Midlands as Green Goddesses fire vehicles crewed by trained troops were sent to deal with the blaze during the firefighters strike and being a Black Country lad (the Black Country is a region of the West Midlands) we all feel part of the huge community of the Black Country and the loss of four children in a fire was felt by everyone. 119 people died as a result of fires since the strike began. These stories were a diversion from my own issues and for a while I could escape my situation by giving deep and sincere sympathies to others who were going through turmoil.

December was a better month than I had expected, I was feeling better and feeling confident that my new prescribed drugs would actually work for me and I had reached my fifteenth birthday and the thought of dying in a seizure was no longer an issue that I was scared of. I was to discover in years to come that SUDEP is a term that refers to sudden unexplained death in epilepsy and this could have been the case with my aunt Sylvia in 1961 rather than the belief of her swallowing her on her tongue and choking to death. And despite the knowledge that my life would never be the same again, I was hoping that I could return to school before the end of July the following year and not go to a boarding school.

January 1978 had passed with no seizures and I was feeling that a weight was slowly being lifted from my shoulders and my medication was actually working for me, my hospital visits was really optimistic too and recent tests were showing that my seizures were being controlled and my road to a normal life was looking promising. My parents felt confident that I could return to my paper round but only if my younger sister agreed to go with me during week days and my dad driving me at each weekend until I was able to deliver my newspapers alone, whenever that day will be.

The customers on my paper round were greeting me on many days and so pleased to see that I was on the road to recovery and the school teacher who had witnessed my seizure on his driveway came out to meet me as I walked towards his front door and as he threw his arms around me,

"OH MY GOD, WHEN WILL WE SEE YOU BACK AT SCHOOL?" he called.

"I am waiting for the hospital to give me the all clear and then I will be back to play you teachers up" I laughed, "It has been a little quieter without you Glyn" laughed the teacher "We have missed you mate" added Mr. Thompson.

And though I was well known for bunking off school (or hopping the wag as we called it) I was really missing being at school, missing my mates and dare I say it - I was missing my teachers too.

February had seen me counting the days that I could be allowed to go swimming but the medical team at the hospital ruled out any chance of being allowed to enter a swimming pool and so I would go to Walsall gala swimming baths as a spectator and watch my friends swimming. The experience of being back in a swimming pool would have been a great feeling but despite not be allowed to swim - I was on the road to recovery and I could be getting my life back in the near future - if only my mum's sister were to have had this treatment back in 1961, if she were to have outlived her seizures - I would have had an aunt who would have been a best friend and a great adviser to help me live my life better with epilepsy. Thankfully for myself, research into epilepsy had moved forward and treatment was more effective since the days of the early 1960's.

Life was getting back to normal and it looked like I had taken on epilepsy and won the battle but not the war, as I was to face a lifetime of taking medication to control my seizures but unsure of being free from seizures in the future. I didn't really look forward to being on medication for the rest of my life but I would rather pop the pills that are prescribed to me than have those seizures return. Despite the good news that my seizures were showing signs of being under control, I still had to face up to the fact that a place in a boarding school could be possible due to the fact that my hospital doctor would not commit his name to a letter that would give me the all clear to return back to school.

On this information I had set up a plan, I started saving more of my paper round money and planned to run away, as far away as I could if the day was to come where I would be sent away. I had done nothing wrong in life but I had served a sentence under 'house arrest' and following that I could be sent to what I envisaged as another prison environment that is called a boarding school - I wasn't going, no way!!

My plan was to jump on a train to anywhere in Devon that had a beach and hotels, I would deliver newspapers to these hotels and bed and breakfast establishments and then work evenings and weekends in the summer seasons - I would earn enough money to rent a place of my own. Eventually I executed my plan and I caught the train from Walsall to Birmingham but then I jumped onto the wrong train at Birmingham new street station and ended up going in the opposite direction to Devon.

When I realised my mistake I quickly jumped off the train at Sutton Coldfield and just wondered around the streets until I reached Sutton park and a cafe at the edge of the park. As I was drinking tea from a polystyrene cup, a voice behind me called,

"Why aren't you at school?" As I turned to see a police officer standing behind me. "I am off school due to illness" I replied, "And what illness is that then?" Asked the officer, "Non of your bloody business" I snapped back in response, "Oh it is my business young man, someone has tried to break into a house up the road and you may fit the description of the offender - come with me" said the officer as he took me by the arm and escorted me into his car.

Now a young lad with an holdall bag that was packed with clothes and food didn't look too good in a situation like this and though I was totally innocent of any wrong doing, I was in deep trouble for betraying my parents trust in allowing me a little bit of freedom and independence.

At the police station I was questioned and my bag was searched and I had no option but to admit the truth about my attempt to run away. "I don't want to go to a boarding school" I sobbed "I don't want to be taken away from my family".

"But you are running away from your family?" puzzled a female officer. "And the point you are making?" I asked, "My point is, you don't want to be taken away from your family but you are running away from your family?" Replied the female officer "A little hypocritical, don't you think young man?"

I just sat there and began to wonder if she had made a good point, she was totally correct in her assumption I guess. On that, a male police officer walked into the interview room, "Okay Glyn, we have called your family to tell them that you are fine" explained the male police officer "We will be driving you to Walsall police station, where your parents will be waiting to collect you".

And so the drive to Walsall from Sutton Coldfield was with an officer in the rear of the car who was trying to cheer me up even though I was not in a happy mood. We reached Walsall police station to which my annoyed parents were waiting. After being told off by the desk sergeant about wasting police time and putting myself in a potentially vulnerable position, I was taken home by my parents and my mum was constantly nagging me all the way home, the lecture of 'what if' was mentioned again - 'What if I had a seizure in a place that I was not familiar with'.. What if ... What if?

The threat of being sent away to a boarding school was really playing on my mind and despite my parents promise to do all they can to stop this happening, I was still in the mindset of having to leave my home - even though it had been my prison in recent times, I didn't want to leave. However, during my hospital visit in April I was informed by my medical team that if I could make it to June without any seizures or any kind of episode, I would be allowed to return to school. This was music to my ears and almost as sweet as listening to my Queen LP's, I was on an high and so confident of my return to school that on some days I would wait at the school gates to meet my school friends at lunchtime and to see if anyone was to give me any hassle when I returned to school.

Simon came to meet me at the school gates one day and we talked about my return to school and how good it would be to be back, "My brother Stuart should be allowed to return to school soon" said Simon as he referred to his younger brother who was suffering epilepsy too. "I never thought I would miss school so much" I sighed as I looked across the school yard "I never thought I would miss him as much as I have" I added as I watched our head teacher walk across the playground towards me.

"Hello Mr. Marston" smiled my headteacher "Do you have time for a chat and a cup of tea?" he asked. "A cup of tea - if you make it a mug of tea you can count me in" I laughed as we walked toward his office.

As we sat in his office and drank the tea that had been bought in by his secretary, the head teacher showed me a letter that had an hospital franking mark on it. "I received this letter today" he said "It's confirmation that you are -

according to your hospital doctor, allowed to return to school" continued the headteacher "You will not be allowed to be doing any physical activities for the time being, especially swimming for obvious reasons" He added as he read the letter.

I just stared back in amazement as tears were filling my eyes but this time they were tears of joy, the joy of realising that my life was to be returning back to normal and as I gulped down another mouthful of tea I looked at the head teacher, "I can't wait to tell my parents" I cried "I don't have to go to a boarding school" I added as I smiled through tears of joy.

On that my head teacher informed me that he was planning to make provisions for me to use a spare office and have teaching assistants to help me with my lessons within the school rather than see me be sent away - he too was against me being sent to a boarding school.

"Your parents should have received this very same letter" explained the head teacher.

"There was a similar letter delivered this morning which is addressed to my parents but they won't open it until they get home from work this evening" I explained.

"I'll tell you what, pretend that you are unaware of this letter and give your parents the pleasure of telling you the good news first so to speak" suggested my head teacher "I will see you in school soon" smiled my head teacher "But promise me that you will wear the correct uniform when you return and you will try not to tease Mr Twain" he added.

"Sir, I have one worry - Mr Twain, we don't see eye to eye and I don't want him to know of my condition, he may use it to bully me" I explained.

"Yes - I am afraid that I have to agree with you on that, I have had to have words with him on more than one occasion about his discipline methods" replied the head teacher "He doesn't need to know any facts- so you get yourself home and wait for your parents to read the good news" he added.

I almost skipped all the way home and sat on my bed listening to my records, I waited patiently for my parents to return home from work. The excitement was building within me as I waited for them to read the letter and call me downstairs to give me the good news but instead of calling me down, my parents ran upstairs and were racing each other to be the first to enter my bedroom - be the first to give me the good news.

My dad burst into my room and waving a letter he shouted, "Have you read this my son?" he laughed, "Obviously I haven't read it, you were the first to open it" I replied, "Oh yeah" He laughed again,

"It's from the hospital" interrupted my mum,

"Yes, the hospital have said that after months of deliberating and reviewing your case - you can return to school" screamed my dad as he threw the letter in the air and hugged me.

I once again broke into tears of joy as my mum joined us in what was now a group hug, we were now recognising that my seizures was to be a thing of the past and something we could put behind us for good. Though my sisters couldn't believe that I would be happy enough to celebrate a return to school but as I explained that it was more of a celebration of a return to normal life and being back at school was to be a symbol of my return to normality. And even though the end of term would be in a short time and I would have a few weeks before breaking up for the summer holidays, that time at school would be a real joy.

My parents decided that as part of my good news we could celebrate by going into town and buying me a complete new uniform (it would save them from having to buy me one after the summer holiday period anyway). Trying on a new blazer and new trousers were a joy, my parents allowed me to have something more fashionable than the standard type of school clothes that the establishment would request I wear. My school shirts were more expensive than the usual shirts that we were to have and my new school shoes were so fashionable, this was made possible by taking my older brother (Audie) along to help me choose my uniform.

I couldn't wait to return to school, I just couldn't wait to walk through those school gates and get back to living a normal life.

Chapter ten

End of term

My return to school was met with great excitement and on the first day of my return I had woke up feeling alive and delivered my newspapers in record speed, the walk to Pool Hayes comprehensive school was an experience you get when you attend a new school for the first time and as I got near to the school the group of friends that I was walking with got bigger as my friends wanted to know why I had been off from school for so long. Giving no explanation and no excuse was to fuel the rumours of myself being sent to young offenders institute and gave me a little bit of 'space' at school (as no-one tried to push the absent issue too much) and so my return to school was to be less of a worry than I had expected, I hated the thought of students thinking I was a jailbird but this eradicated any worries of bullying and protected me from the fear about my epilepsy being discovered by anyone else that was not in the King Charles pub on the evening of my seizure. Paul, Craig and Mickey attended Willenhall comprehensive and were friends I could have done with at that moment though.

Returning to school was met with the clash of personalities between myself and Mr Twain, Twain was the head of P.E. - also the head of our year and was not too pleased that he was kept in the dark about my prolonged absence from school. Mr Twain would stop me in the corridors or the school playground and question me about the reasons for being away from school for so long. In fact he would stop me anywhere he bumped into me and harass me at every possible chance. "Rumours are going around this school that you have been in Borstal" he called out loudly as to let other school kids listen to his accusations "What were you convicted of- mugging old age pensioners I bet?" he questioned.

"I have not been in Borstal and I have never mugged anyone in my life so back off" I would shout in defence.

"So where have you been all this time?" he replied,

"NON OF YOU BLOODY BUSINESS" I shouted back as I squared up to this bullying teacher.

"Go on Glyn, hit me - hit me and I will have you arrested for assault and you will be returned to Borstal" He grinned as he tried to provoke me.

"I ain't been to Borstal" I shouted as I walked away from him.

And this story of being in a Borstal was getting on my nerves but it had a good side too, school friends were trying to stay on my good side and not upset me as they feared the reputation that came with being in Borstal. The school kids who had a bad reputation for bullying were now trying to be my friends and I needed this status to help protect me from the possibility of being a target of bullying because of my epilepsy, this new but unwanted status was to help me protect me from any rumours that could occur around my illness.

My return to school had seen a few teachers welcome me back and one teacher in particular was to welcome me back more than anyone else, Mr. Thompson was the teacher who had witnessed me in a seizure that one morning on his driveway and as requested by the head teacher, he told no-one else and kept my secret to himself. I was in total relief for this trust from a teacher, Mr.Thompson had not told any other teacher as he didn't want to risk this news becoming public knowledge by any teacher who may have mentioned it with the risk of being overheard. Of course Miss Williams knew of my condition but she never made a huge fuss of my return to school as she didn't want to arouse anyone suspicions of my condition.

Over the course of the first week of retuning back to school I was introduced to Stuart by his brother Simon,

"This kid will look after you Stuart" said Simon as he introduced us.

"Are you the other kid with epilepsy?" Whispered Stuart.

"Shut your mouth" I whispered back "We keep that thing a secret".

"Oh, sorry mate" replied Stuart "I am pleased that I have someone to talk to about the condition and I am not alone".

"We don't talk about 'it' at school, do you understand?" I whispered back through gritted teeth "If anyone gets to find out about why I was off school for so long - we will not be friends, understand?"

Simon reminded his brother that in a few weeks time he would have left school to start an apprenticeship and for the last year of Stuart's time at school, I will be the only one to protect him from any bullying - but I could only do that if I were not to be bullied myself and I could only guarantee that by not allowing anyone to know that I was on medication to control epilepsy. Stuart was under the impression that if folk knew of my epilepsy they would be more understanding and therefore be sympathetic to his epilepsy, I disagreed with his theory as I had witnessed how cruel folk can be when faced with someone who is epileptic and I was not prepared to take the risk of anyone at school knowing my story.

Unfortunately for me, the hospital doctor had agreed my return to school but with a few exclusions and those were to exclude me from swimming, athletics- well any physical activity until further hospital visits were to conclude my fitness to return to any kind of physical activities. I hated this rule that my medics had put on my agreement to return to school for I missed playing football and I missed swimming.

My head teacher was so instrumental in allowing me to go to hospital visits without raising suspicion and he would personally grant permission for me to leave school for any hospital visits I had to attend, I was so grateful for this gesture and it raised no suspicion from my school friends.

However, I was unaware that Mr Twain would storm into the head teachers office on many occasions and demanded to know why I had been allowed to leave school. "As Glyn's head of year, I think I have a right to be informed of anything surrounding Glyn's situation" requested Mr.Twain.

But the head teacher requested that Mr.Twain leave his office and mind his own business which angered Mr.Twain even more. And so I felt protected, I felt safe and secure in the environment at school.

I didn't know how Stuart was coping at school as I stayed out of his way but I did mention to his brother Simon that I would be angry if his brother were to tell anyone about his condition by describing mine. All I needed to do was to keep my illness away from school chums until the end of term in a few weeks time and then the long summer holiday from school would be upon us and the return to school in September will see that my school friends would have forgotten about my long absence.

On one hospital visit my parents presented me with a medical I.D. bracelet, it was a beautiful silver chained bracelet with a silver capsule to the middle and the word 'EPILEPSY' engraved on the front of the capsule and even though it was a wonderful gesture, I couldn't wear it - especially at school for it would be no different than tattooing 'I'M AN EPILEPTIC' on my forehead and so I refused to wear it.

My dad was so pleased that he had bought me a bracelet that would see me get medical help as soon as I needed it should I fall into a seizure but I had to remind him that the stigma surrounding epilepsy is likened to someone having leprosy and you wouldn't expect a leper to be given a warm welcome in any school environment. And so I kept the bracelet in my bedroom and would promise to wear it if we were away on holidays. "Do you know son" sighed my dad "There may come a day when folk in your situation will be able to announce that they have epilepsy and folk will be more understanding of what you are going through".

"Do you think that one day I will have the courage or stupidity to admit to being epileptic?" I laughed, "To stand in front of a crowd and shout out about my epilepsy would be the same as a circus ring master calling out - ROLL UP, ROLL UP AND COME SEE THE FREAK - THIS FREAK WILL SHAKE HIS BODY SO FAST AND SO VIOLENTLY WHILE HIS LIPS TURN BLUE AND HE FROTHS AT THE MOUTH - HURRY, HURRY ROLL UP - that day will never happen".

"You never know, not only will you stand up proud and loud and admit to having epilepsy - you may put your name to a book about the condition" my dad proclaimed,

"Never, never - that will never happen, me admit to being epileptic by writing a book - you are joking?" I scoffed as I dismissed the idea. "Well, you never know" replied my dad.

Back at school and any problem I was to have would not be from any potential bullying from students but bullying from one particular teacher - Mr Twain. This teacher was so determined to know of my reasons for being absent from school for so long and if it wasn't a reason of being locked away for any crimes, then what possible reason could I have had? I couldn't risk him finding out about my epilepsy because he would have used it to intimidate me and to bully me as much as he could. This was a teacher who hated children and he definitely hated his job- in fact, he hated children so much that he tolerated his job so he could make children's life a misery.

And one day was to come that would give him his moment to embarrass me, a Thursday afternoon to be exact - an upcoming swimming lesson which would see myself and a few other students lining up with bits of paper that would have reasons to be excused from class written on them. As Mr Twain walked along the line he would read each piece of paper out loud (in a bid to embarrass the student) and then decide whether to excuse or make them take part in the lesson.

As Mr Twain approached me, he looked me up and down and said.

"Why am I not surprised to see you trying to skive swimming" he grinned, "I'm not trying to skive, I have a letter that excuses me" I replied,

Snatching it from my hand and reading it out loudly for everyone to hear, "This letter does not say why you should be excused from lesson" He stated, "Its a letter from the hospital" I protested, "I can see it's a letter from the hospital that states you cannot part take in lessons, but it does not say why you need to be excused" grunted the bullying teacher "Now if you were to tell me why you should be excused, tell me what is wrong with you - I may consider excusing you - and don't use snow blindness or the time of the month as an excuse either" He added as to reference my previous attempts to wind him up with stupid reasons to be excused from class. At this point I was about to give in - bite the bullet so to speak and admit to Mr Twain about my condition but only in the privacy of his office.

"Sir, can we talk about this alone please?" I requested "Can we go in your office - now?"

"WHO ARE YOU TO MAKE DEMANDS ON ME - WHO THE HELL DO YOU THINK YOU ARE?" Bellowed the teacher, "WE HAVE NO SECRETS HERE, YOU CAN TELL ME HERE IN FRONT OF CLASS OR GO IN THE POOL - YOUR CHOICE" He bellowed out in a bid to embarrass me.

I could feel my blood boiling and I tightly clenched my fists as I became so close to punching him in the face but I thought better of it. I looked around the corridor that had my school mates lined up against a wall and thought that going in the swimming pool against hospital advice is better than admitting to having epilepsy in front of most of the students who were waiting to enter the changing rooms. Now my medical team at the hospital were in agreement to allowing back at school but they did not want the responsibility of me swimming until they had conducted more tests to show that my condition was now well and truly under control - what do I do?

"Sir, if you phone the headteacher in his office, he will tell you that I am to be excused" I begged, "But will he tell me why you are to be excused"? Asked Mr Twain. "I don't think so" I sighed as I dropped my head.

"Well I won't be bothering him then will I?" Scolded the teacher as he made me stand up straight "Spare trunks in the lost property bin in my office - sort yourself a pair and get undressed" he ordered.

As I rifled my way through the lost property bin and searched for a pair of half decent trunks I could hear him picking on Stuart who had presented him with a similar hospital letter that I had and to my horror, Stuart was about to admit to his illness. I peered from the door of the office and looking at Stuart I shook my head and mouthed the words "NO, DON'T DO IT".

Stuart, like myself did not give a reason and therefore he was not excused from swimming and joined me in looking for a pair of swimming trunks from the lost property bin, "My dad will go mad- he will go mad when he finds out what that teacher has made me do" moaned Stuart.

"My dad will punch his lights out, you wait and see, my dad will be here tomorrow and he will deck Mr Twain for doing this to me" I growled in anger, (deck being a term to express that someone will be knocked flat on their back). "I tell you what, we could make a run for it to the head teachers office and report him" Stuart suggested.

But then Mr Twain appeared in the office to see why we were taking so long to choose a pair of trunks. "Sir I can't wear any of these, they have not been lost - they have been thrown away" I pleaded.

"You wear something or you swim naked" he shouted.

"Okay, have it your way then - I am going in naked" I shouted as I walked into the changing room. I was hoping to call Mr Twains bluff and hope that he would take the option of giving me a detention rather than risk me streaking around the swimming pool.

"The last thing I want to see is an ugly git like you walking naked around my pool" snarled Mr Twain "Put these on - now" he grunted as he threw me a pair of tatty swimming trunks.

Stuart had followed me in a pair of swimming trunks that looked like a pair of shorts a boxer would wear- these were clearly too big for him. As we entered the poolside all the students were in hysterics as they laughed at the two kids wearing ill fitting trunks.

"QUIET YOU NOISEY LOT" bellowed Mr. Twain who was unaware of a student that was looking through the windows and that student was Simon (Stuarts brother) who was horrified to see that I was being forced to go into the pool but even more horrified to see that his younger brother was standing by the side of the pool too and therefore began to run into the pool area. As I stood there with Stuart standing next to me I could hear Stuart quietly mumbling and see his body start to shake and so I called out to the teacher, "SIR, SIR" I bellowed.

"Shut up Marston, you ex-con" replied the teacher, "But sir..." I shouted.

Before I could finish my sentence 'SPLASH' as Stuart just flopped into the pool and fearing the worse, I dived in after him. Stuart just sank to the bottom of the pool and his body was shaking violently as I tried to pull him up to the surface, I could hear the muffled sound of Mr Twains voice shouting to us to get out of the pool as I struggled under the water. The time underwater was only moments but it felt like time had slowed down and everything was happening in slow motion. Stuart was shaking so badly as he hit the floor of pool and I tried frantically to lift him to the surface.

As I surfaced to the top of the water I screamed out for help only to be assisted by Simon who had come running into the pool area and dived into the pool partially clothed. Other students dived in too and we all managed to push Stuarts shaking body onto the side of the pool and after hearing the commotion that was going on, a few other teachers came running to our assistance. Mr Twain tried to help Stuart by putting him the recovery position and check his breathing but Simon screamed, "GET AWAY FROM HIM, GET AWAY - YOU ALMOST KILLED MY BROTHER" Simon scream hysterically as he feared for his younger brothers life.

I ran into the changing room and cried my heart out, for I had never witnessed anyone in a seizure before and the reality of what my family had witnessed each time I had a seizure had suddenly hit me, I was totally shocked at witnessing someone in an epileptic seizure.

I punched the walls again and again in anger but not just in anger at a bullying teacher but in anger of an illness that is so cruel and so unforgiving. As I punched the walls my rage got worse and my punches harder for I could not comprehend that my family had to witness the sight that I had just seen when I was having my seizures, "Is this what I have subjected my family to?" I thought to myself, "Is this the horrific scenes that they had to deal with each time I had my episodes?"

I eventually sat down and as I sat there trying to calm myself down, my class had all been ordered back into he changing room to get dressed as the lesson had now been cancelled. I stood up and punched the walls in anger and frustration once again and as Mr Twain walked into the changing room to allow the paramedics to do their job at the poolside I approached him and pushing my face into his I screamed "YOU BAST…" but I was interrupted in mid sentence by a teacher who was sent to get me from the changing room.

I was requested to get dressed and go to the headteachers office to explain why I went against advice issued by the hospital and by my head teacher, why was I in the pool?

As I stood there in the headteachers office with water dripping from my clothes (I had been given trunks to wear but no towel to dry myself with), I explained to the headteacher about being forced to either take the lesson or having to admit my condition in front of other students. We were now joined by a police officer who came to the school when an ambulance was called, I had to make a statement there and then with other students being questioned by other officers in the changing room. But as I was giving a statement I spotted my dad's car pull up into the school driveway, apparently the rumour of the incident in the pool had spread around the school and my younger sister thought it was me who had a seizure and therefore she ran to a phone box just by the school gates and called my dad at his place of work.

"Oh no - my dad is here and he looks angry" I sighed as I watched my dad march across the school yard. I could hear my dad shouting in the reception area as he was demanding to know the whereabouts of his son. I ran out of the headteachers office and to the reception area, "I am okay dad, I am fine" I called out as I was now joined by the police officer and the headteacher.

"Look at you, just look at you" sighed my dad in relief that I was looking okay "What happened and why were you in the swimming pool?" he asked, "I think we need to discuss this in private" requested the head teacher as he started to walk toward his office.

When I repeated my story, my dad was furious and wanted to confront Mr Twain but fortunately the police officer had confirmed that Mr Twain had been taken away to the local police station for further questioning and was not on the school premises. My dad would have been jailed for murder or manslaughter if he had got his hands on Mr Twain for putting me in a dangerous situation. I had never seen my dad so emotional as he explained, "I came here today expecting someone to tell me that my son had been taken to hospital and is fighting for his life" explained my dad as his eyes were welling up "That teacher could have killed a kid today" he added.

"I need to ask as to why this teacher wasn't informed of the students medical history and why he wasn't told of their exclusion from physical activities?" Asked the police officer.

"There had been reports of this teachers behaviour in the past where he had harassed a student at a different school by letting the student's health issues become public knowledge and in turn, it was to lead to the student being a target of bullying" explained the headteacher "And though nothing definite could be proved against Mr Twain, he was transferred to this school" added the headteacher.

"And he tried to bully my older son, how many times did I have to come to this school and threaten him to leave my son alone?" my dad angrily stated as he referred to my older brothers time at the school.

"Under the circumstances, I made the decision to keep Glyn's condition and Stuarts to just a few members of staff. Let's face it, they had letters from the hospital that stated they were to be excluded from physical activities and those letters should have been respected without question" added the headteacher who was clearly showing signs of remorse.

"My request" I called out "My request - I begged that Mr Twain would not be told of my condition" and as I continued with the feeling of guilt, I cried out with tears yet again rolling down my face "I forced Stuart to keep quiet about his epilepsy and if I hadn't… he wouldn't have been in the pool, I have to take some of the responsibility".

But what about Stuart? His secret was out and no sympathy was shown toward him as the epilepsy jokes started all over again - the carpet **fitter**, the **fittest** swimmer in school and so on. It was a blessing that he wasn't at school to hear the jokes that referred to epileptic fits (dogs have fits, humans have seizures). We didn't get to hear about Mr Twain but rumours were rife about the fact that he claimed that had he been informed correctly of our medical condition he wouldn't have allowed us in the pool, he put the responsibility and the blame onto the school's headteacher. There were rumours that Mr Twain had taken early retirement but I like to think that he was unable to get a job at any other school and his early retirement was forced upon him. The weeks that followed were difficult for me as I had to endure jokes about epilepsy - Stuarts epilepsy and those jokes were cruel, so cruel in fact that I wouldn't dare put them into words. I obviously would refuse to laugh and indicated that those kind of jokes were not funny at all - epilepsy is not funny, it is serious and a condition that can take a life, it took my aunts life and almost took Stuarts.

Finally the school bell signalled the end of a day and the end of term and as we look forward to the six weeks summer break from school, I recalled that almost a year ago I suffered my first seizure and was to experience more. My life was to change forever but I could live my life with regret and self pity or I could put it behind me and live my life to the full, the medication that I was prescribed was to be taken indefinitely and I was to have a life of being on medication to control epilepsy.

The following term was to see Stuart returned to school, but a different school - he was unhappy about spending his final school year relocating to a new school but the bullying he would have received at his old school would have been too much for him to deal with. As for me I started the new term and my final year at school trying to catch up on the education I had missed in the previous year. I was to apply for the army but I got refused for obvious reasons and this was to be the life ahead of me, certain jobs that I could never do because of my health issues - but I was pleased that I made it past my fourteenth year and beyond my fifteenth birthday and (unlike my aunt Sylvia) I have a lifetime to look forward to and boy am I going to live it.

2021

Looking back

From time to time I return to Pine needle croft, the cul-de-sac where my first seizure happened and try to work out what actually happened that day - the day of my first seizure. I park my car opposite the shopping precinct in Stroud avenue and walk through the short alleyway to the cul-de-sac, I stand there (at the end of the alleyway) with the vision of that day in my head and I look for anything that will tell me of what really happened that morning. I still recall the residents coming to my aid and the ambulance taking me away but I have no memory of waking up, collecting my newspapers and cycling into the area on that day - the day that changed my life. Forty four years later (as I write this paragraph) I firmly believe that there were no impact to my head caused from a fall from my bike and was not the cause of my condition - I would have put my arms out to cushion my fall as I had done on previous falls from my bike and therefore I was 'out cold' before I hit the ground - it was a seizure that caused me to fall from my bike. I still yearn for some recall from that morning of my first seizure, I still feel that the blank space in my life - that blank space in-between going to bed one evening and waking up in a cul-de-sac the next morning needs to be filled in - but it never will.

Despite being on medication for life to control epilepsy - I have been luckily enough to be free from seizures for over 43 years as I write this paragraph but this has come with limitations on my life - jobs and promotions I couldn't apply for due to medical reasons were to pose a huge disappointment but despite this, I have kept a promise to myself to live my life to the full and so far I have ran across the Grand Canyon from the North rim to the South rim, ran in road races of 155 miles non stop, broken world records for running on treadmills and ran in over 100 marathons around the world and folk see me as a picture of health and fitness (unaware of my medical past).

I keep taking the tablets and being on medication for life to control my epilepsy is not an issue - for those tablets have given me my independence, my freedom and my right to have a happy life. The happiest part of my life now is being able to tell the world that I am on medication to control epilepsy (something that I never thought would happen).

God bless everyone who is living with epilepsy.

Glyn x

Printed in Great Britain
by Amazon